THE TRIUMPH OF THE CROSS
BY
FRA GIROLAMO SAVONAROLA

Translated from the Italian

EDITED, WITH INTRODUCTION
BY THE
Very Rev. FATHER JOHN PROCTER, S.T.L.
PROVINCIAL OF THE DOMINICANS IN ENGLAND

The work ... on The Triumph of the Cross is a witness to
my faith"
— (Letter of Savonarola to Pope Alexander VI.)

LONDON
SANDS & CO.

DUBLIN
M. H. GILL & SON
1901

ISBN: 978-0-9819901-1-8

Printed and Bound in the United States of America.

Published by:
St Athanasius Press
133 Slazing Rd
Potosi, WI 53820
1-608-763-4097
melwaller@gmail.com
http://www.stathanasiuspress.com

Email is the best way to reach us.

Check out our other titles at the end of the book!

Nihil Obstat
Joannes Procter, O.P., S.T.L.
Die Martii 27, 1901.

Imprimatur.
Herbertus Cardinalis Vaughan,
Archiepiscopus Westmonast,
Die Martii 28, 1901.

INTRODUCTION.

Savonarola was a speaker rather than a writer. His was the eloquent ministry of the living word, rather than the calm apostolate of the lifeless pen. He was more at home when standing in the pulpit of the Duomo in Florence, facing the panting, throbbing crowd, numbering thousands, who, with itching ears and thirsting souls, drank in his every word, as though the words were dewdrops from heaven, than when sitting at the little table — which is still preserved in his lowly cell at San Marco — holding in his emaciated hand a nerveless, passionless pen. His great master-intellect and his large sympathetic heart seemed to long to pour out their rich pent-up treasures, freely and without stint, through the channel of his eloquent tongue; whereas the hand that would perpetuate his thoughts, by stamping them upon paper, at times seemed palsied. Out of the abundance of his heart his mouth preferred to speak. Still he wrote sometimes; — it was generally, however, under moral compulsion, being impelled to do so by circumstances which he could not control. He was accused of error by those, or to those at a distance; his advice was sought by others who were far away — defense or counsel had to be committed to paper. For a time he might not sway the masses, as he would, by the irresistible magic of his burning words; then we have the apostolate of the pen. He retired to the seclusion of his monastic cell, and wrote, as his zeal prompted, his message to his fellow-men. Many of his treatises —
short ones for the most part — exist. We have his five books — we might call them chapters, they are so brief — on "The Simplicity of the Christian Life"; a treatise on "Humility"; an exposition of the "Our Father," and another of the "Hail Mary"; commentaries on

some of the Psalms; an explanation of the Mass, and of the ceremonies of the Holy Sacrifice; certain rules for good Christian living (composed when he was in prison), and a number of other letters and booklets. But perhaps the most notable, as well as the most useful, of his writings are the four little "Books, "as he calls them, which these words are to introduce to the English-reading public, and which he himself styles, in the Prologue or Introduction to the First Book, a defense of" the glorious TRIUMPH OF THE Cross "over" the profane and foolish babble of worldly-wise Philosophers".

Of St. Philip Neri, the Apostle of Rome, who was ever staunch in his loyalty to the memory of the one who, for a time at least, was the Apostle of his own native Florence, it is said, that this was one of his favorite books. The Saint's biographer. Cardinal Capecelatro, writes :"It is well known that Philip often read the writings of Savonarola, especially The Triumph of the Cross, and that he used them for the instruction of his spiritual children. There are still preserved in the Vallicella, among the books which belonged to St. Philip, and which were given by him to the Congregation, five of Savonarola's works." 1

The history and object of The TRIUMPH OF THE Cross, which may be considered the most important of the works, if we may so call them, of the great Florentine Reformer, is given by Echard, the Continuator of Quetif, in his Scriptores Ordinis Praedicatorum 2

The Triumph of the Cross is (he tells us) an accurate work, and one approved by all learned men.

Savonarola undertook it for this special reason, namely, that he might clearly show what were his real feelings as regards the Catholic Faith and the Apostolic See; and that he might refute the calumnious accusation of heresy and schism, which had been laid to his charge by his adversaries. It begins thus: "The glorious triumph of the Cross over the worldly wise and over wordy sophists, etc."It is divided into four books, of which the first treats of the existence, nature, and providence of God, and proves the immortality of the soul of Man. In the second the author shows, by various arguments, how the Christian faith is in accord with truth and reason. He proceeds, in the third , to point out that there is nothing intrinsically, or extrinsically, impossible in the chief mysteries of the Christian faith and that they are not, in any way at variance with reason. The fourth book is mainly devoted to an exposition of the truth of the religion taught by Christ.

It shows that the vagaries of philosophers, astrologers, idolaters, Jews, Mahometans, and heretics are absolutely opposed to reason.

This work Savonarola wrote in Latin, and it was printed at Florence in 1497 in quarto. It was reprinted there, in quarto, in 1524, and afterwards in Paris at the Ascension Press, in octavo, in the same year. Next it was published at Basle by Henrici-Pietri, in 1540, in folio. Then, more accurately, thanks to the zeal of the famous John Balesdens, by John Maire at Lyons (1633), in duodecimo. It was also reproduced at Rome by Cardinal S. Onufrius Antonius Barberini, brother of Urban VIII., at the Propaganda Press, in duodecimo, without any date. Finally, another edition was issued at Grenoble, in 1666, under the care of the famous companion of Stephen Mency.

But since many of Savonarola's adherents were unable
to obtain a copy, and were unacquainted with the Latin
language, in which it was written, in accordance with
their wishes he translated it into the Etruscan tongue,
not indeed (as he warns his readers in his introductory
letter), word for word, or line for line, but merely giving
the sense and the pith of each chapter, and sometimes
(to make a special point the more convincing to his
readers), omitting some passages and adding others. 3
He says that he did this advisedly, lest it should be purposely, and maliciously, mistranslated by another. This
was edited at Florence in the year 1497, in quarto, and to it
a Preface was written by Domenico Benevieni, a Florentine
noble, who was Canon Theologian of St. Laurence's in
the same city. In this Preface Benevieni defended the
author in a very able manner. This version was reprinted
at Venice, by Bernard of Bindoni, in 1531, in octavo, and
again, in octavo, in 1547. 4 It must be noticed that the
seventh chapter of the Fourth Book of the Latin edition
was taken out of its place, and inserted, by Theodore
Bibliandrus, in his collection of works written against
the Mahometan errors. It is to be found in the second
part of the Basle Folio editions of 1543 and 1550, under
the title:"Commentatiuncula Savonarolse Mahumeticam
sectam omni ratione carere ostendens".

In his Etude sur Jerome Savonarole, the Reverend Pere
Bayonne, O.P., 5 adds to what we have already said, that
the brother of Urban VIII., Cardinal Onufrius Antonius
Barberini — a Capuchin — wishing to vindicate his
(Savonarola's) innocence, left by will, dated 23rd of
August, 1646, 500 gold crowns to bring out a reprint of The
Triumph of the Cross, and his commentary on the Miserere.

The heirs of the Cardinal gave this commission, as we have seen, to the Propaganda Press; and these two works accordingly appeared. They were sufficient to dispel all the illusions of those who still suspected the author of heresy and of hostility to the Holy See.

The same writer also quotes M. Perrens as saying that the Society of Jesus printed The Triumph of the Cross in their Annals of the Propagation of the Faith (vol. 2., p. 211). The most recent edition is one which appeared in 1899. It was published, both in Latin and Italian, on parallel pages, at Siena, under the title "Trionfo DELLA Croce di Fra Girolamo Savonarola, edito per la prima volte, nei due teste originali Latino e Volgare, per cura del P. Lodovico Ferretti de' Predicatori". I would here acknowledge, with thanks, my indebtedness to the Reverend Editor of this valuable edition. He has kindly put his work at my service in editing the translation which these words introduce to the English reader.

This is the book which is now presented to the reader in an English form. It is the first time, as far as I can ascertain, that it appears, in its entirety, in English. 6 I say in its entirety. In reality, there are two paragraphs omitted in the eighth chapter of the Third Book, the omitted paragraphs being denoted by asterisks. The reason of the omission is, that the author treats of a physical question of some delicacy; and, as, since Savonarola's day, the views of scientists on the subject have changed, it has been designedly left out. I may add, however, that the omission does not in any way affect the author's argument. 7 I am fully aware that a work was published, some years ago, purporting to be an English translation of the four books, and that the Rev. Father Lucas, S.J., in his recent biographical study, Fra

Girolamo Savonarola, calls his readers' attention to it as ''an English translation of THE TRIUMPH OF THE CROSS''. 8 I have the book before me as I write, and I cannot agree with the learned Jesuit in accepting this mutilated and eviscerated English version as a translation of Savonarola's Triumph of the Cross, nor do I think that the Florentine Dominican would, were he able to do so, give either his Nihil Obstat or his Iinprimatur to the work as a reproduction of his own words, or as the full profession of his own creed. The title of the book is "The Triumph of the Cross, by Jerome Savonarola, translated from the Latin . . . by O'Dell Travers Hill, F.R.G.S."; it was published in London in 1868. It is NOT a translation of The Triumph of the Cross. It is, apparently, only a translation of certain portions of the book which would prove palatable to the class of readers for whom the "translation "was clearly intended. Whole chapters have been dropped out, evidently without the slightest compunction, certainly without the least explanation. In some of the chapters which appear, lengthy passages have been omitted without the shadow of hesitation. Truly, it is Hamlet without the Prince of Denmark. It is no more a translation of the great Dominican's famous defense of his orthodoxy — as The Triumph of the Cross was intended to be — than the garden fence of a suburban London villa is a reproduction upon English soil of the Wall of China, or than Primrose Hill is an English replica of the Alps. If the books of Catholic Apologists are to be "translated" in this way, what is to prevent a Unitarian from giving us in English an edition of the Bible without any allusion direct or indirect, to the Blessed Trinity? Or what is to hinder an Agnostic from reproducing the Gospels in our mother tongue, without any reference to the Central Figure, around whom the whole of the sacred writings revolve?

The "translator" tells us in his Preface that "this book is free from all sectarian feeling or prejudice". No doubt it is. But why? Everything "sectarian" in The Triumph of the Cross has been left out in the "translation". He speaks of "its freedom from all sectarian spirit, from all scholastic quibbling"; and concludes that "its close consecutive reasoning, its earnestness, convince us that its author was a man far in advance of his age". If the unbiased reader will peruse the pages of this translation, from first page to last, from the opening chapter of the First Book to the closing chapter of the Fourth, and compare the doctrine of the four books with the teaching of any book written by any recognized Catholic Apologist, in any tongue, in this twentieth century, he will find that, in a sense, the words of the Preface are true, and that. Savonarola, writing in the fifteenth century, was" "advance of his age'; that he was one with the Catholic writers of this twentieth age. If he will pursue his reading still further, and compare the true TRIUMPH OF THE CROSS with the works of the Catholic Apologists of the middle, and earlier, nay the earliest ages, he will find that Savonarola was behind his age, as well as being in advance of it. There are no '' ages" in the history of the Catholic Creed of the Catholic Church. Like Jesus Christ, the Church and the Church's teaching are "yesterday, today, and the same forever". 9 Savona-rola's teaching in this profession of his creed — the creed in which he lived, in which he died, and which he preached through life and with his dying breath — is the creed of the Catholic Church in all places and in all times."This is My Covenant with them, says the Lord. My Spirit that is in thee, and the words

that I have put in thy mouth, shall not depart out of
thy mouth, nor out of the mouth of thy seed, nor out
of the mouth of thy seed's seed, says the Lord, from
henceforth and forever."' 10

The translator of what I cannot but call the Pseudo
Triumph of the Cross, but which he ascribes to
Savonarola, professes on the title page that it is '' translated from the Latin"; and in the Preface he assures
his readers that "this translation has been made from
a valuable copy, printed with all the abbreviations
peculiar to Savonarola's manuscript, found in the
Archives of Sion College". Where, then, does the
fault lie? Who is responsible for the omissions? 11 Is
the defect — or are the defects, for their name is
"Legion"— in the original, or in the "translation"?
Let us see. There is only one Latin copy of The
Triumph of the Cross in the Sion College Archives,
and, as the translator says, it is "a valuable copy". It
lacks the first page; otherwise it is complete. The loss
of the title page, however, matters little, as the edition
is recorded at the end of the book :"Venumdatur in
aedibus Ascensianis. Typog. Ascensiana, MDXXIIII."
Truly" a valuable copy ,"printed in Paris by a certain
J. B. Ascensianis in the year 1524, only twenty-six years
after the author's tragic death. It is not the first
edition. This, as we have seen, appeared in Florence
in 1497, the year before he died. Still it is an early
edition. There is another copy of this Ascension
Press edition of 1524 in the library of the British
Museum. A third copy, belonging to the library of
the Dominican Fathers at Woodchester, lies on my
desk as I write these words. It is a small octavo
volume bound in vellum, and besides The TRIUMPH
OF THE Cross, it contains several other treatises of

the Florentine Dominican. The inscription at the end, with the date, corresponds to the Sion College copy. The space at my command will only allow me to call attention to two or three discrepancies between the original, the "valuable copy" found in the Archives of Sion College, and the book which claims to be a translation.

In the original Latin edition, the Third Book contains eighteen chapters; in the translation only fifteen chapters appear. There is no explanation given, either in the Preface or in the body of the work, of the reason of the omission, nor is it stated that these three chapters are omitted. The chapters which are absolutely ignored in the pseudo-translation are those which appear in the original, and in this present translation, as chapters 15., 16., and 18. If the reader will refer to them, he may perhaps form his own opinion as to the reason of the omission from what purports to be a translation. These chapters contain what the translator would pro-bably call "sectarian" teaching; they embody the "sectarian spirit, "from which, he tells us, The Triumph of the Cross is free. The first of the three omitted chapters treats of the Sacraments, and teaches that there are seven, even as does the Catholic Catechism of today. Following the argument of St. Thomas, the author shows the need of each, of the seven Sacraments, from the analogy between the life of the body and the spiritual life of the soul In the following, or sixteenth chapter, which the translator, on his own responsibility, evidently puts under a ban of excommunication from an English home, Savonarola treats of what the scholastics call "the matter and form" of the Sacraments, and explains, in terse and clear words, the meaning and object of each of these seven channels of grace to the soul. This chapter is "sectarian" indeed. Hence, we may presume, its eradication, its being pulled up root and branch from English soil; hence its elimination from English pages; hence its absolute extermination, as far as English readers are concerned. Savonarola wrote it in Latin, and reproduced it in Italian, but we will have no popery and no popish doctrine in our pure English tongue! We have it, however, at last, in this translation, as we have had it from the beginning in the chapter of the original to which I allude. Baptism, Confirmation, Holy Eucharist, Penance (or Confession), Extreme Unction, Holy Orders, Matrimony — all are there, with their object, their meaning, their "matter and form," as the scholastics would call their component parts, their mode of administration, and their effects upon the human soul in time and in eternity.

Finally, in the third of the proscribed chapters — the eighteenth in the original work — we have a dissertation on the Ceremonies of the Church. Savonarola shows with what wisdom they form part of the Church's discipline, and how they answer to a demand of the soul of man in his worship of the Most High. The author explains, too, some of the practices of the Catholic Church, which, in our days, as in his own, are often misrepresented or misunderstood.

The unprejudiced reader may draw his own conclusions as to the reason of the omission of the three chapters from the book we have been referring to, and which appear, probably for the first time in English, in the pages which follow this Introduction. The Twenty-fifth of the Thirty-nine Articles of the Anglican Creed declares :"There are two Sacraments ordained

13

of Christ our Lord . . . Baptism and the Supper of the Lord". Savonarola says there are seven. The Twenty-eighth Article professes that "transubstantiation . . . cannot be proved in Holy Writ; it is repugnant to the plain words of Scripture". Savonarola, on the contrary, holds that the Catholic doctrine can be proved, and that it is clearly taught in Holy Writ by Jesus Christ the Divine Teacher. The Thirty-fourth Article attaches little importance to ceremonies, and calls in question the need of outward uniformity in the services of the Church. Savonarola has an entire chapter written in their defense and explanation, in which he speaks of crucifix and images, of devotion to the Mother of Jesus, of the consecration of churches, of lighted candles, of sacred vessels, and even of holy water. What then? The Articles are right; Savonarola must be wrong; he must be "sectarian". Then leave out the sectarianism; omit the chapters in which he treats of subjects which are distinctly and essentially Catholic, It is the old story. They will make Savonarola a Protestant, or, at least, a herald of Protestantism, a precursor of Luther and Calvin, a harbinger of the Reformation, whether he will or no. Whereas, as every reader of his history and writings must know, he was of Catholics the most Catholic — Catholic in life, Catholic in death, Catholic to the heart's core.

I must leave it to the calm unbiased judgment of the reader to decide whether this kind of translation is fair; whether it is just to the memory of the great Dominican whom so many. Catholics and non-Catholics alike, profess to revere; whether it is just even to the English-reading people, to the vast majority of whom original works written in Latin or Italian are sealed books, and who have consequently to depend upon the fidelity and

accuracy of a translation. If the translator had professed
to give an expurgated edition of The Triumph of the
Cross; if he had told his readers that he had eliminated
everything that was "sectarian"; if he had undertaken to
give selections from the work, in defense of Christianity; if
he had professed to reproduce, in more modern English, the
translation published by the Cambridge University Press in
1661, to which I have referred — this we could understand;
but to call a book with several chapters ruthlessly
discarded, "THE
Triumph of the Cross translated from the Latin"
— this, assuredly, it is beyond the power of words to
condemn. The translator of the Cambridge edition of
1661 — as we may readily understand both from the
date and the place of the publication — omits the
identical passages omitted in the edition of 1868 — those
which I have referred to, and others to which I shall refer,
— but he is candid and fair in so doing. He
prepares the reader for this in his Preface or Dedicatory
Letter, to which he appends his initials, J. W. B. "I
know"(he writes) '' that you will not disdain to look
upon him (Savonarola) in this English Dress, wherewith
I have attired him; nor blame me for having cut off
some few shreds, that he might, with more credit, appear
amongst us. , . . You will approve of my choice of this
author, who lived in the thickest darkness of popery. "Not
so, however, the "translator" of the English edition of
1868. He suppresses whole paragraphs and entire chapters
without note or comment. Moreover, he assigns no reason
for so doing.

One further reference, and I have done with this so-
called translation. In the original edition of A.D. 1524
we find in the Fourth Book nine chapters. In the
mutilated English version we find also nine. No

chapter, it is true, is bodily omitted from the Fourth Book. One chapter, however, has come under the reckless and unscrupulous pruning knife of the translator; evidently, again, because it ran counter to his religious views, or the preconceived ideas of those for whose benefit he was translating. The sixth chapter of this Fourth Book, which professedly treats of the doctrine of heretics, is in reality a dissertation on Church government, and a plea for visible Church unity under one visible head. After instancing, by way of analogy, the unity of bees under one queen, and the unity of the members of the human body under one head, the author goes on to show the need there is of one Chief Ruler in the Church. He quotes the prophet Osee, and also the well-known words of our Lord about the "One fold and the One Shepherd". He then proceeds to argue that Christ was the visible Head of the Church when on earth, adding that when He ascended into Heaven, He would not leave the Church" without any earthly head," seeing that in such a case it would become a prey to divisions, confusion, and dis- order; and therefore He_ said to Peter, ''Feed My sheep"."Thou art Peter, and upon this rock," etc. And again :"I will give unto thee the keys of the Kingdom of Heaven," etc. All this we find word for word in the English version which we are considering. Savonarola then continues — AND THE WHOLE OF THE FOLLOWING WORDS ARE EXCLUDED FROM THE PSEUDO-TRANSLATION:

— ''It can not, however, be supposed that Christ conferred this dignity on Peter alone, to the exclusion of his successors, since He Himself has declared that the Church should endure forever in the order which He had established. Speaking to His disciples, and, in their person, addressing all the faithful, He said: ' Behold I am with you

16

even unto the consummation of the world ' (Matt, 28:20).

And again, by the mouth of Isaias, He said : ' He
shall sit upon the throne of David and upon his kingdom; to establish it, and strengthen it with judgment
and justice, from henceforth and forever ' (Is. 9:7).
These passages clearly indicate that the office., confided by to St Peter, being highly expedient
and necessary to the Church, should, by an unbroken
succession, be guaranteed to her forever. Hence it follows
that, as Peter was chosen by Christ to be His vicar
and the shepherd of the whole Church, all his successors
must inherit his power. And, as the bishops of Rome hold
the place of Peter, 'THE ROMAN CHURCH MUST
CONSEQUENTLY BE THE "MISTRESS AND RULER
OF ALL CHURCHES, AND THE WHOLE BODY OF
THE FAITHFUL MUST LIVE IN UNITY WITH THE
ROMAN PONTIFF. Whosoever, therefore, disagrees in his
teaching with the doctrine of the Roman Church withdraws from Christ, following crooked ways. And, as all
heretics dissent from the teaching of the Church, they
have all declined from the right way, and are unworthy
of the name of Christians. For by heretics we mean
such as, falsifying the words of Holy Scripture and
choosing a religion for themselves, do obstinately
persevere in their error.

"Again, Truth, as is often said, mates with truth, and
all truths confirm each other. Now heretics disagree
so entirely among themselves, that they have scarcely
one point in common, nay, rather they bespatter each
other with abuse; they present no solidity of argument.
This fact alone proves how far they have wandered
from the Truth. But the doctrine of the Roman
Church, in all matters affecting faith or morals, is one;

17

and Catholic doctors, though almost innumerable, never dissent nor desire to dissent from it."

Every syllable of this profession of Savonarola's faith in the supremacy of the successor of St. Peter is expunged in the""translated version. There are no asterisks to show that words are left out. There is no footnote, no word in the Preface, to explain the unpardonable liberty of the translator. A comma is put after the words "loosed in heaven," and the translator continues, — as though this were the author's continuation, —"from which we may see that Jesus Christ," down to the words '' He shall sit and rule upon the throne of David," etc. The entire passage about the successor of St. Peter, "Hence it follows," is summarily omitted from what purports to be a translation.

I have nothing more to say, except, in justice to Savonarola, to enter a protest against the book to which I have been referring being considered a translation of The Triumph of the Cross. If I have dwelt at length upon this subject, it is only out of respect for, and in justice to the memory of, one for whom I have a sincere veneration, and who has so often, and so unjustly and unjustifiably, been represented as being wanting in loyalty to the See of Peter, of being" a forerunner of Luther, "and" a harbinger of the Reformation". 12 It is by such methods as the one against which I am protesting that these accusations against the Catholic loyalty of Savonarola have been apparently substantiated. It is by the persistent repetition of them that they have been perpetuated. "Here" (they say)" is a book of his which professedly gives us the articles of his creed. It is absolutely unsectarian. There is nothing distinctively Catholic in it. Nothing which any non-Catholic could object to. There is not a word about the seven Sacraments, about Confession, Extreme Unction, the Mass, Ceremonies, and above all about the Pope being the successor of St. Peter in the government of the Church!" And yet the reader will find all these doctrines of Catholic belief clearly and luminously treated. He will find an explicit profession of faith in all the vital and crucial articles of the Catholic Creed in the volume which is now presented to him, together with the author's" reason for the hope which was in him". For Savonarola was ever mindful of the admonition of the Chief Apostle," being always ready to satisfy every one that asks you a reason for that hope which is in you". 13

The Triumph of the Cross ought to "satisfy" the English mind upon the subject of his orthodoxy forever. The Triumph of the Cross gives the "reason" of it, in clear and concise and unmistakable words. It is difficult to see how anyone who has read it, could entertain the shadow of a doubt about the author's loyal devotion to the Church of which he was a faithful child, or of his belief in the teaching of the one whom he proudly called his "Mother". Indeed, it is impossible to see how, with the evidence of this book before him, any man could hesitate for a moment as to his belief in the unwavering loyalty of Savonarola both to the Church and the Church's teaching, and to her divinely appointed visible Head.

St. Peter, the Dominican Martyr, as he fell under the blow of the assassin's sword, wrote with his own blood on the ground the word CREDO. Savonarola, the Dominican Apologist, has written CREDO in large letters over every page of THE Triumph of the Cross. It is a history of the religious opinions of his times. It is more. It is the exposition in writing of the doctrines which he preached, with such incomparable eloquence, from beginning to end of his apostolic life. It is his clear and uncompromising profession of faith to all time. It is his solemn anathema to heresy, of which, nevertheless, men have sometimes dared to accuse him. This book ought to lay that ghost of an accusation against the Florentine Reformer forever and forever.

It proclaims Savonarola's Catholicity beyond denial or doubt. It was intended to be his defense of the faith. It was written as his profession of belief. It was to be his Credo in life, and the echo of his belief after his death, when his voice was still, and he could no longer protest, as he did with such vigor in his lifetime, against his false accusers. In the Preface which he wrote to the Apologeticum Fratrum Sancti Marci — published probably the year before his death — he says: "Three accusations have been brought against me: (1) That I have taught a doctrine which is not true {perversum dogma) ... to this I have already replied, and my orthodoxy will be clearly seen in my work, The Triumph of the Cross, which will shortly appear". In a letter to Pope Alexander VI., written from St. Marco, Florence, on the 22nd of May, 1497, 14 he writes: "The work which I shall shortly bring out on The Triumph of the Cross is a witness to my faith; and from it can be seen if I have ever taught heresy, or in any way opposed the Catholic faith". This book is his testimony unto all time.

The late indefatigable and zealous champion of Savonarola, Professor Paolo Luotto, wrote a goodly volume, to which he gave the title : Il Vero Savonarola, et II Savonarola di S. Pastor. The English people, as well as Signor Pastor, have had a Savonarola of their own. The Savonarola of the English is a Savonarola created by novels and romances, by non-Catholic and anti-Catholic histories and biographics, by prejudiced enthusiasts, and unscrupulous translators. This faithful English translation of the whole of The Triumph of the Cross— for which we are indebted to an anonymous but graceful as well as faithful pen — will, let us hope, reveal The True Savonarola — the Savonarola of fact and not of fiction, the Savonarola of history and not merely of romance, the Savonarola as mirrored in his own words, and not as misrepresented and distorted, and rendered beyond recognition by many who, whilst professing to extol him, and to add luster to his name, have, in reality, belittled him, and sullied his fair fame.

JOHN PROCTER, O.P.

Postscript. — Since writing the foregoing INTRODUCTION the recent valuable and interesting work. The Story of Florence, by Mr. Edmund G. Gardner, has come into my hands. I have much pleasure in transcribing the following note, which occurs on page 128: "Professor Villari justly remarks that 'Savonarola's attacks were never directed in the slightest degree against the dogmas of the Church of Rome, but solely against those who corrupted them'. THE TRIUMPH OF THE CROSS was intended to do for the Renaissance what St. Thomas Aquinas had accomplished for the Middle Ages in his Summa Contra Gentiles. As this book is the fullest expression of Savonarola's creed, it is much to be regretted that more than one of its English translators have omitted some of its most characteristic and important passages bearing upon Catholic practice and doctrine, without the slightest indication that any such process of * expurgation ' has been carried out." J. P.

TABLE OF CONTENTS.

THE TRUTH OF FAITH MANIFESTED BY THE TRIUMPH OF THE CROSS.

BOOK I.

THE TRUTH OF OUR FAITH MADE MANIFEST IN THE TRIUMPH OF THE CROSS.

Written by Fra Girolamo Savonarola of Ferrara, of the Order of Preachers.

PROLOGUE.

The glorious triumph of the Cross embraces so many mysteries that, in attempting to unfold them, and thus to silence the profane and foolish babble of worldly-wise philosophers, I am undertaking a task far above my powers, and can trust only to the help of the Lord.

It would seem mere waste of time to discuss and analyze our Faith, based as it is upon the miraculous works of our Saviour Jesus Christ, which are patent to the whole world, and upon the teaching of venerable theologians. Nevertheless, there are nowadays men living in such bondage to vice, that, even in the light of the noonday sun, they grope in darkness, and scorn the marvels of heavenly science. I, therefore, on fire with zeal for the House of God, intend, for the sake of the salvation of these misguided men, and in order to rouse them from the slumber that oppresses them, to recall to their memory the things of Christ, which they have forgotten and thrust from their hearts.

Our Faith cannot be demonstrated by natural prin-ciples and causes. Nevertheless, the past and present events of Church history afford arguments in support of our religion so convincing that no logical mind can reject them. At the same time, no one believes that Faith itself depends upon these arguments, seeing that it is "the gift of God; not of works, that no man may glory" (Eph. 2:8, 9). We make use of these arguments indeed;

but we do so in order to confirm the faith of such as waver, to prepare unbelievers for the reception of super-natural light, and to enable the faithful to confute the arguments of irreligious men; and thus, by exposing their folly, to undeceive the simple and unlearned who have been misled by them.

This use of human reasoning does not detract from the value of Faith; for the axiom that faith proved by argument has no merit, refers only to the faith of such as refuse to believe without proof They who, being enlightened by God, embrace the Faith without proof, and who then, in order to strengthen their own belief and that of others, investigate the grounds of their faith, deserve commendation, and obey the precept of St. Peter: "Sanctify the Lord Christ in your hearts, being ready always to satisfy everyone that asks you a reason of that hope which is in you" (1 Peter 3:15). In this book we intend to be guided by reason only. We shall not, then, appeal to any authority, but shall proceed as if we had no belief in any one in the world, no matter how learned he may be. We shall rely solely on reason. Such a mode of procedure must, surely, satisfy everyone who is not absolutely foolish.

Chapter 1

HOW BY MEANS OF VISIBLE THINGS WE ARRIVE AT THE KNOWLEDGE OF SUCH AS ARE INVISIBLE.

The senses, in which all our knowledge originates, take cognizance only of extrinsic corporeal accidents. Our understanding, on the other hand, is enabled, by its subtlety, to penetrate to the substance of natural things, and thence to rise to the knowledge of such as are invisible and immaterial. Thus, by the investigation of the substance and properties, the order, the causes and the activities of visible things, we are led, by little and little, to the understanding of invisible substance, and, at length, to the "knowledge of the Divine Majesty; just as, by means of the external accidents and operations of man, we arrive at the understanding of his soul, and of its invisible parts. Philosophers, from the contemplation of the universe — of the heavens with their magnificence; of the elements with their divers motions and operations; of the variety and activity and individual perfections of the things composed of these elements; and of the wonderful harmony and greatness and beauty of this visible world — have raised their eyes to gaze upon invisible things, and to investigate (so far as might be) their nature and properties. 15 And, as these philosophers have understood that natural things are the work of God's hands, and are the means of arriving at a knowledge of His infinite power and glory, we likewise desire to show that those things which have been seen, and are still witnessed, in the Church of God, are Divine works, by which we may attain to the knowledge of the glory and Infinite Majesty of our Saviour Jesus Christ, who is unseen by us.

Sages of old were wont to marshal before their eyes
all the visible things of the universe. Thus, the wonderful works of nature constrained them to acknowledge
God as the First Cause of all things, and natural
phenomena as the creation of His unerring wisdom.
We, in like manner, must bring together before our
minds all the wonderful works of Christ, whereby we
desire to prove that He was the First Cause of all things,
and that all His doings proceeded from God, who can not
err. We would not be understood to say, that these
proofs cause Christians to believe; for they are established in their faith by the supernatural light of God
(otherwise, their belief would be, not faith, but opinion).
But such testimonies confirm us in our Faith, and prove to
our adversaries that we believe, not lightly, but
thoughtfully and with deliberation. In order the better
to bring the works of Christ, which are continually being
performed in the Church, before the eyes of men, we will
describe them under the figure of a triumphal car, the figure
of the entire universe.

Chapter II

HOW THE TRIUMPH OF CHRIST TESTIFIES TO THE TRUTH OF OUR FAITH.

As the power, wisdom and goodness of God are infinite, they could not be manifested (save most imperfectly) in one creature. Therefore, philosophers have been wont to contemplate the Divine Majesty, revealed in the harmony of the universe, resulting not from one but from numberless creatures, which, on account of their necessary dependence one on the other, can with ease be considered simultaneously. In like manner, we cannot understand the power and wisdom and goodness of Christ by contemplating only one of His works. We must recall to our minds all the wonders which He wrought. Thus we shall be constrained, not on one count alone, but for many reasons, to acknowledge His Divinity. For, should we not be convinced by one of His miracles or arguments, we cannot (unless we be obstinate) fail to be persuaded when we consider His works and teaching collectively. But, although it be easy, by reason of their mutual dependence, to consider all the marvels of nature collectively, it is not equally easy to contemplate all the works of Christ at once. It has, therefore, occurred to me to present them under the figure of a triumphal car, a similitude easy of comprehension to the feeblest intellect.

Let us, then, represent to our minds a four-wheeled chariot on which is seated Christ, as Conqueror, crowned with thorns, and bearing the marks of His wounds, thus showing that it is through His Passion and death that He has overcome the world. Over His Head shines a light like a triple sun. This represents the Blessed Trinity, which illuminates His Humanity and the whole Church with unspeakable splendour. In His left hand Christ holds the Cross and the instruments of His Passion, in His right the Old and the New Testaments. At His Feet are the Host and chalice; vessels of balsam and of oil; and the other symbols of the Sacraments. The Blessed Mother of God, the Virgin Mary, is seated beneath her Son. Around, and below her, are vessels of gold, silver and precious stones, filled with ashes and bones of the dead. The Apostles and Preachers go before the car, appearing to draw it. They are preceded by the Patriarchs, the Prophets, and innumerable men and women of the Old Testament. The chariot is encircled by the army of Martyrs, forming as it were a crown. They, again, are surrounded by the Doctors of the Church, bearing open books. Around them, again, circles a countless multitude of virgins, of both sexes, adorned with lilies. Behind the car follow innumerable men and women of all conditions — Jews, Greeks, Latins, barbarians, rich and poor, learned and simple, small and great, old and young; all of whom, with one accord, are praising Christ. And, all around this multitude, gathered from the Old and from the New Testaments, are the serried ranks of the enemies of the Church of Christ — emperors and kings; princes and men in power; sages; philosophers; heretics; slaves and freemen; men and women; people of every race and of every tongue. Whilst around them lie idols, prone and broken, heretical books burnt, and all sects, and every false religion confounded and destroyed.

Now the chariot which we have described symbolizes a new world, from whence shall spring a new philosophy. Its first cause, and the invisible things which become known to philosophers by means of visible things, are represented by the figure of the Blessed Trinity, True God, above the Head of Christ which represents His Manhood, and by the innumerable company of Angels and Blessed Spirits, who are all unseen by us. We must arrive at the knowledge of these spiritual beings by means. of the visible beings grouped around the chariot. And, just as philosophers teach that the heavens are the cause of all things produced beneath them, so we say that, after the Divine Majesty, the chief cause of grace and salvation is the Passion and Cross of Christ. Beneath the firmament are the elements, which derive all their activity from the heavens; so to the Passion of Christ succeed the Sacraments of the Church, deriving all their power from It.

The elements are followed in the natural world by particular causes, such as seeds and the like. In our triumph, the seed is represented by the teaching of the Gospel, and by the works and example of the Saints whose relics repose in honour in glorious tombs, and the memory of whose merits and holy lives produces continual fruit in the Church. Particular causes are figured by the Apostles, Patriarchs, Prophets, Martyrs and Doctors; who, while they lived, regenerated, by their teaching, the whole world to Christ. Lastly, as in the natural order effect follows cause, we represent effect by the countless men and women who have been converted by the example and the preaching of the Saints.

But, as in nature, every movement is from one contrary to another, and the generation of one thing is the destruction of something else (for in all reproductions there are two opposing forces, of which the stronger prevails), so, in the spiritual generation, Christ and His elect have vanquished His enemies, represented by heresy, prostrate around the triumphal car. The four wheels of the chariot signify the four quarters of the world, so marvelously enlightened by Christ, and by

Him brought into subjection.

And, as philosophers, having before their eyes the
order of the universe, and considering the wonderful
effects of nature, did, by searching for their causes, as-
cend gradually from the lower to the higher, and attained
to the knowledge of invisible things and of the Divine
Majesty; so, if we examine attentively the works which
Christ has performed, and still does perform, in His Church
(represented by this chariot), we shall begin to be filled
with wonder, and shall diligently seek the
cause of those works, and thus shall, gradually, rise to
the knowledge of invisible things, and of the Divine
Majesty of Christ.

CHAPTER III.

CONTAINING CERTAIN FUNDAMENTAL AND IRREFRAGABLE PRINCIPLES.

If an argument is to be conducted satisfactorily, the disputants must agree with each other about some point. For, if they disagree on every point, there will be no possibility of discussion. They may, or may not, of course, think alike on matters of minor importance; but they must agree about certain principles, which are so generally accepted that no one denies them. We must, therefore, take up our position on certain acknowledged principles. We cannot argue with one who denies them; for he who refuses to accept first principles is unreasonable. First, then, we are all agreed that Jesus Christ was crucified by the Jews, and was afterwards, throughout almost the entire world, adored as God, as we Christians adore Him, This fact is admitted by Jews, heretics, Mahometans, Greeks, Latins and barbarians; the belief in it has never died, but has been handed down, from generation to generation. Testimony to this conviction is, further, forthcoming in the books written in every language and diffused throughout the world, and in the ruins of Christian churches to be found in every land. These are proof positive that there is not a spot on the face of the earth where Christ has not been worshipped, or is not still adored", or where, at least, there is not some knowledge of Christianity. Hence, even unbelievers speak of Christ as the God of the Christians.

If, therefore, no reasonable being will controvert that which is made manifest by the books and the monuments of every nation; he who should deny that Christ was slain by the Jews, and was afterwards adored as God throughout the world, must be so foolish, that argument with him would be waste of time. And, if it be acknowledged that the adoration of Christ has been universal, the same must be said of the confession of the Blessed Trinity, and of the Eucharist, the veneration of the Cross, of the Virgin Mary, and of the Saints. The same evidence demonstrates, further, that the Apostles, who were at first fishermen, preached the Cross of Christ; that they were preceded by the Jewish people, the Patriarchs and Prophets; and that they were followed by the glorious Martyrs, the venerable Doctors, the spotless Virgins of the Church, and likewise by an untold number of monks and priests, both regular and secular.

Finally, we must remember that, although the tyrants and the philosophers of the world have fought against the Church, idolatry, nevertheless, has been destroyed, heresy has been extirpated and even the Roman Emperor has been brought into humble subjection to the fisherman, and that the heretics and their heretical books have been destroyed. These things being so well known as to need no proof, we shall presuppose them, as philosophers are wont to presuppose the truths of science.

For they are acknowledged, not only by Christians, but by nearly every people and in almost every country, yea even by Indians and innumerable Mahometans, amongst whom exist certain proofs of our faith, who admit that Christ has reigned amongst them and has worked miracles, and who, although they themselves are in grave error, yet punish severely all who blaspheme the Christian truths. Since, then, these truths are so clearly manifest, they can be gainsaid by none but such as are foolishly obstinate.

CHAPTER IV.

ANSWERS TO THE OBJECTIONS WHICH MAY BE BROUGHT AGAINST THE FOREGOING PROPOSITIONS.

But perhaps someone will say: If your assertions be true, surely it is strange that no pagan historian or orator should make any mention of them; But that they, who minutely describe the wars and other doings of men, should pass over in silence the works of Christ, which are so much greater and more wonderful. Exception must be made in the case of certain historians, who, wishing to refute Christianity, have rendered testimony to its truth.

To these objections we reply, that it is false to say that pagan historians have not written concerning Christ and His Church. For not only have many authors, both Greek and Latin, treated fully and eloquently of His praises, but many of them have been converted to His Faith, and have propagated it by their preaching and their writing.^ And, if our objectors should reply, that they allude not to those who, after their conversion, have written about Christ, but to those who have remained in their errors; our answer is, that our Faith has confirmed its converts to such a degree, that not only have they written of the praises of Christ and of the Church, but they have not hesitated to shed their blood for His religion. For not only have those brought up from their infancy as Christians written in behalf of their Faith, but likewise innumerable and well-known men, of different nations, have embraced the truth in their more mature years. And it is a much more convincing proof of the truth of Christianity, that its converts should have died for it, than it they had remained heathens and had written volumes in its praise. What wonder that proud and incredulous men should have neglected to narrate the works of Christ, when, beholding His miracles, they refused to accept His Faith!

There are two further reasons why pagan historians have not written in praise of Christ. One reason is the providence of God; the other their own blindness. God moves all things, both corporeal and spiritual, and cares for all things; and no one can move himself to write, unless he be inspired thereto by God. Therefore, the heathen historians have not written of Christ, because God did not move them to do so.

Now, Divine Providence did not inspire them to write for three reasons. First, God ordinarily makes use of fitting means to achieve an end, and the pagan philosophers who were stained by infidelity and other vices, were not fit to write of the pure and holy works of Christ and of His Church.

5econdly, as Christ is Truth itself, and came into the world to give testimony of the truth, it was not seemly that men, who, like the pagan poets, orators and historians, perpetuated lies and fables and praised the foulest deeds, should have defiled the pure truths of Christ by writing of Him.

Thirdly, the heath en orators had none but the eloquence which springs from natural reason; they sought rather to magnify themselves than to declare the truth. As the works of Christ, on the other hand, are above natural reason, it is evident that these pagans were not fit men to treat of them.

Another cause which prevented the heathen writers from bearing witness to Christ was the blindness, caused by their sins, especially pride and vain-glory, which so completely darkened their hearts that they took no account of the miracles wrought by Christ, such as the restoration of sight to the blind, the raising of the dead, and so many other wonders, which none but God could perform. Furthermore, as the heathen authors had been nurtured, from their infancy, in the worship of their gods, and in idolatrous fables, they, naturally, entertained a hatred for Christianity, the sworn enemy of idolatry. They would not, therefore, write anything in favour of the Church, both on account of their detestation of her, and for fear of exciting the displeasure of the tyrants who persecuted the Christians.

Again, we must remember that these poets and orators, by their egregious flattery, cultivated the good graces of princes, in the hope of being rewarded by them; and, as they knew that there was nothing to be gained from Christians who loved truth and professed poverty, it is not surprising that they did not write about Christ. Now, on the contrary, when the Church possesses temporal dominion, there is no lack of poets and orators to sing the praises of her princes and prelates; they often even mingle with their eulogies many things which are not true. If the Gentile authors did not espouse the cause of Christ, we need not go far to find the reason of their silence.

CHAPTER V.

THE MODE IN WHICH OUR ARGUMENT MUST BE CONDUCTED.

Since we attain to the knowledge of the invisible by means of the visible, we must understand, that there are some among the invisible things of God which we can know by the natural power of our understanding, and by means of natural things. Such things are, the Existence of God, His Unity, His Simplicity of Being, and other truths of this sort, to the knowledge of which philosophers have attained. But there are others among the invisible things of God, which we cannot discover by means of human reason. This is not very strange, seeing that, even among men who are equal by nature, philosophers can understand high and subtle matters, of which children and simple persons must remain in ignorance. This being so, is it to be wondered at that in God there are secrets, which no created intellect can investigate? We cannot understand many of the things which we meet with every day; how then shall we comprehend God, who infinitely surpasses all things?

The Divine things which our natural reason is not competent to discover are those which we believe by Faith, to wit, the Trinity and Unity of God, the Divinity and Humanity of our Saviour Jesus Christ, and other truths of the like nature. But, although we cannot prove these truths by natural effects or human arguments, we may, nevertheless, make ourselves very sure of them by their supernatural effects. For, just as, by natural effects, we know that the propositions, "God exists," and "God is One and Infinite," etc., are true, and yet by means of them know not God as He is, nor behold His Substance; so also, by means of supernatural effects, we can certify ourselves of the truth of such propositions as "God is Three and One,""the Son of God is both God and Man". Yet we cannot understand, nor see these truths, as they are in themselves.

As nature precedes grace, we will first treat of those invisible things of God which we are competent to investigate by means of their natural effects, and after-wards of those which can be known by their effects which are supernatural. The truths of the first category, however, we will consider very briefly, since Catholic theologians and philosophers have discussed them so thoroughly, as to leave no possibility of doubt.

CHAPTER VI.

THE EXISTENCE OF GOD.

If we do not mean to stultify our whole argument, we must begin by proving the existence of God. What do we mean by God? All men use this name to designate that which is higher and more excellent than all other things. Some call this Highest Being the Prime Mover of all things; others call it the First Cause and Principle, or the Highest Good and Supreme Truth. But, whatsoever God may be called, if His name expresses the highest and superexcellent nature, His existence must be acknowledged. This is admitted even by philosophers. It is of His existence that I wish briefly to speak.

Philosophers have proved, most effectually, that everything that moves is moved by something else. Even though men and brutes move themselves, there is in them, one thing that moves and another that is moved; for the body cannot move when abandoned by the soul. And, since every movement under the heavens depends on the movement of the heavens, there must be some substance that moves the heavens. Now, does that substance Itself move, or does it not? If it does not move, it must be God, who moves all things, but is Himself immovable. But if the substance move, it must then be moved by something else. Now, is that something else immovable, or is it also moved? If it be moved, who moves it? If we continue this chain of argument, we shall see that there must either be one First Mover, or else an infinite series of movements with no First Mover.

The second hypothesis is philosophically absurd. For if there be no First Mover, on which other motors depend, nothing could move, and no order would reign among the highest things. There must, then, be one supreme Mover, whom we call God.

We can deduce a similar argument from the causation of things. Everything in the world is caused. Nothing can make itself. Since then many causes concur to the same effect, and one thing is always prior to another, we must either assume an infinite series of causes, or believe in One Supreme Cause, whom all men acknowledge as God.

Again, amongst natural things we see that one thing is always more true and more perfect than another. This could not be the case, did it not approximate more closely to some Supreme Truth and Perfection. We must, therefore, agree that there exists some Supreme Being. This can be no other but God.

Again, we see how, in the natural order, unintelligent beings proceed by the right means from their beginning to their end. This cannot happen by chance, since they always, or almost always, act in the same manner. There must, then, be some Intelligence that directs them. What can this Intelligence be save God?

To these arguments we may further add, that no natural inclination can be futile. Now all men are naturally inclined to believe in God. From the beginning of the world until now there has never been (as we know from their superstitious rites and sacrifices any nation so rude and barbarous as not to believe in a God. Since, then, this belief has been common to every era, and to every nation, it must be based on natural instinct. Again, we see how men, when in danger and deprived of human aid, will, instinctively, invoke the assistance of

God. This is another proof that belief in His existence is natural to the human soul.

CHAPTER VII.

GOD IS NOT A BODY, NOR THE FORM OF A BODY, NOR IS HE A COMPLEX SUBSTANCE.

No true philosopher entertains the slightest doubt that God is not a body, nor the form of a body, nor a complex substance. It would be impossible that God should be a body, seeing that He is the immovable Mover of all things; for one body, unless it first move itself, cannot set another in motion. Again, as spirit is more noble than body, God, were He a body, would not be the noblest of all beings, neither would He be the Supreme Ruler, since the body is governed by the spirit.

We must further hold, that God is not the form of a body, as the soul is the form of the human body; because that which exists of itself is far more noble than that which exists in others. Consequently, as God is the most noble of all things. He must exist in Himself, and not in any body. Again, things composed of matter and of form are more perfect than matter alone and form alone; for the simple reason that the whole is always more perfect than its parts. If, then, God were the form of a body, there would be something more perfect than He; for the combination of matter and form would be more perfect than form alone. It would further follow that God could not act by Himself; since, as form has no being without matter, it cannot operate without matter. Hence, as God would need others for His operations, He would not be the First Cause.

It is, likewise, evident that God is not a complex Being, but Pure Act and Simple Substance; for every complex being depends on others, and composite bodies depend on those that are simple. Since, therefore, God is the First Cause, independent of all others, and the one on whom all things depend. He cannot be a complex Being, but must be Simple Act. Again, were He a complex Substance, He could not be the First Supreme Being in the universe; for complex bodies do not pre-cede their parts, but result from them; and the union of these parts could not take place, had not some first cause preceded them. We must conclude, therefore, that God is Simple Substance and Pure Act. 17

CHAPTER VIII.

GOD IS THE PERFECT AND SUPREME GOOD, AND IS OF INFINITE POWER; HE IS IN EVERY PLACE; AND HE IS IMMUTABLE AND ETERNAL.

If we believe (as we must) that God is Pure Act, we are also compelled to acknowledge that He is perfect, the Supreme Good, Infinite in Power, Ubiquitous, Immutable and Eternal. The greater the simplicity of an immaterial thing, the greater, likewise, will be its perfection. God being absolutely devoid of complexity, Pure Act, and Simplicity Itself, we must also conclude that in Him is supreme Goodness and Perfection.

Again, as everything possesses greater power and virtue, in proportion as it is raised above matter, and becomes more formal; God, as Pure Act, being supremely elevated above all imperfection, and in the highest degree Formal, must be infinite, and infinitely Powerful, And, just as particular effects are reduced to particular causes, universal effects must be reduced to universal causes. Now, being is the most universal of all effects, because it is common to all things; it must therefore proceed from an Universal Cause, which is God, who is the Cause of being, not only by giving it, but also by preserving it. And, since it is necessary that when the cause operates, it must join its power to its effect, God, being His own Power, must be united to the being of all things. Therefore He must be intimately in all things, because being is more closely allied to nature than any other thing.

God, being indivisible, must be in the whole universe, and wholly in each of its parts. He is likewise immutable; because everything that changes must needs be composite, and God, being Pure Act, can know no change. He must necessarily also be eternal; because, were He not eternal. He would be mutable, having beginning and end; and thus He would not be God, but a being dependent on other things, and consequently not the First Cause.

CHAPTER IX.

GOD IS ONE.

It is clear that there can be only one God, not many gods; for the Divine Nature being Simplicity cannot communicate Itself outside Itself. Every nature which is communicated to others, suffers composition, because it must suffer diversity of being. It is impossible therefore, that the Divine Nature should be shared by other beings.

If there were more gods than one, they would differ from one another; and the cause of their difference would be, either some imperfection, or some perfection. Were the cause an imperfection, the god that had it would not be God, because God is wholly perfect. Were the cause a perfection, the God that had it not, would, for the same reason, not be God. Thus there cannot be more gods than one.

A third proof of the unity of God lies in the fact, that all things in the universe are most excellently ordered. This perfect order would not be the work of many: it must proceed from one. Among animals, such as bees and cranes, we see one ruler directing a multitude of subjects. And since art imitates nature, in the best human governments we, likewise, see power vested in one head,otherwise the government could not stand. In like manner, since the government of the Universe is of all forms of government the most perfect, we see that in it there is but one Supreme Lord and Ruler, who is God.

CHAPTER X.

GOD KNOWS ALL THINGS PERFECTLY, AND ACTS OF HIS OWN WILL, AND NOT FROM NATURAL NECESSITY.

It is clear, from what has been said, that God knows all things. We see in the natural order, that those beings that are capable of knowing have a larger and more capacious nature than those that have no cognitive faculty. For, not only do they know their own form, but, being of a nature superior to matter, their cognitive power is able to receive the forms of other things. Hence the cognition of every cognitive form is ample and perfect, in proportion as that form is superior to matter. God, then, being Pure Act, i.e., superior to all matter and all potentiality, must possess the highest degree of cognizance, and the most complete understanding of all things.

God does not understand as men understand, i.e., by receiving the likeness of things into His understanding. For, being Simple Substance, His wisdom and His understanding are His nature; and, being wisdom itself He knows all things of Himself. And, since the power of God is naught but God Himself, and He is likewise wisdom itself, His wisdom must comprehend His power; and as His power is infinite, His wisdom must alike be infinite.

Some men entertain the foolish opinion that God knows super terrestrial things determinately, but that His knowledge of earthly things is confused and general; in other words, that man knows more things, or has a more perfect knowledge of them, than has God. Yet, even in merely natural things, the greater and more perfect the power, the more things it embraces and penetrates; and the more elevated a human intellect, the greater is its range of understanding, and the more exquisite its subtlety. Since, then, the Divine understanding is super eminent, and infinitely perfect, it must necessarily penetrate all things to their innermost being. And, since it is Immutable and Eternal, it is necessary that it should have perfect knowledge, not only of all things past, present and future, but also of all those which might ever be called into being. Moreover, this knowledge has not only existed from all eternity, but continues in the present, and will endure forever.

We must, further, affirm that God acts, not from necessity, but by His Understanding and Will. Nature acts in a certain order without understanding it; and, as there can not be order without intelligence, the operations of nature must be governed by some superior intellect. Now, as the intellect which governs is higher than the nature which is governed, and as God is the First Principle of all things, it is evident that He must act, not by natural necessity, but by Understanding and Will.

That which acts by natural necessity is drawn by its nature to produce an effect as far as possible similar to itself. Now, as God is Infinite Power, He would, therefore, were He constrained by natural necessity to act, produce infinite things — which would be an impossibility. God produces things according as they exist in Himself as in their Cause. Even as a house exists in the mind of an architect who builds it by means of his intelligence and will, so God also creates all things by means of His Intelligence and Will.

CHAPTER XI.

THE PROVIDENCE OF GOD EXTENDS OVER ALL THINGS.

If our foregoing statements be true, there is no room for doubt that the Providence of God extends over all things; not merely over natural things, but over even the smallest human action.

The word Providence signifies a knowledge of the order of things, with an intention of reducing them, by fitting means, to their end. Therefore, as God is Supreme Wisdom, to Him it belongs to order and dispose of all things, as the First Cause, who acts on all things by His understanding, determined by His free will. And, as He is Supreme Wisdom, whose attribute it is to order all things aright, we must acknowledge that in Him is perfect Providence over all things.

Philosophers have never hesitated to recognize Divine Providence in the marvelous operations of Nature. The disordered and confused state of human affairs has, how ever, presented a difficulty to them, and has led some among them to deny the Providence of God over human things.

But, if we reflect, we shall see that it is foolish to deny the Providence of God in the conduct of human affairs, as well as in the order of nature. For the more noble things are, the more perfectly are they ordered; therefore, as man is the noblest of all beings, his operations must be ordered.

Again, as the wisest men take more thought and care

for the things which are nearer to their end, than for those which are more remote from it, so, as man is nearer to God (the end of all things) than are natural things, it would be impossible to believe that, while Providence governs nature, it does not extend to human affairs.

Further, Divine Providence proceeds from the love of God; and the more God loves a creature, the greater is His Providence over it. Since, then, by giving to man a more perfect nature and a higher order of operation than He has given to natural things, God has shown that His love for man is greater than His love for natural things, we cannot doubt that His Providence, likewise is exercised in human affairs.

Another proof of what we say lies in the fact that it is natural (as we see in the case of animals with their young) for all causes to exercise a certain providence over their effects. But as all secondary causes act only in imitation of God, the First Cause, it is evident that He must exercise Providence over all things, and especially over man, who is His noblest effect, and whom He loves more than other natural things.

We must further remember that, if God does not extend His Providence to man, it must be, either because He cannot do so, or knows not how to do so, or else will not do so. Since He is Infinite Power and Infinite Wisdom, it is vain to say that He cannot care for man, or knows not how to do so. To say that He will not do so, is to derogate from His Infinite Goodness; for none that is good spurns his own work, and no cause despises its own effect. Neither would it be a righteous work to care for imperfect things, and not for perfect ones. When even every good and wise man cares diligently for human affairs, how shall we say that the God of Infinite Goodness takes no heed of them?

CHAPTER XII.

THE END TO WHICH MAN IS GUIDED BY DIVINE PROVIDENCE.

Since it is the work of Divine Providence to move all things to their end, and, since all things have their different proximate ends, they must be moved by different means. Irrational things are led by natural instinct, and are rather ruled by others than self-governing. Man, however, having free will, can take thought for himself, and is moved towards his end by God, in such a way that he governs himself, by working together with God. It is, therefore, essential that he should diligently strive to discover what is the last end to which he is destined by Divine Providence; and what the means are whereby he must attain to it; that so he may be enabled to order his life conformably to the designs of God.

Philosophers have studiously endeavoured to search out the End of Man. In course of time, as their reasoning became more profound, and their investigation approached nearer to the truth, they concluded that the end of human life is the contemplation of Divine things. For this alone is the proper operation of the human soul, and it is not directed to any other thing as to its end, but is desired for itself, and unites man to God. Again, man so far suffices in himself to this operation, that for it he needs but few external aids.

This, in fact, is the end of all things that pertain to

man. For all natural things are ordered for the body of man; his body is ordered for his soul; and all the powers of his soul serve to this contemplation, which requires that calm and freedom from passion which art and civil government are intended to procure for us.

It is thus evident that all things, both natural and artificial, are ordered to this contemplation, as to the last end to which Providence moves all men by means of moral virtues. It influences them, however, in such a way, as to leave them the freedom of their will. It is, likewise, clear, that if they will cooperate with the impulse of Providence, they will, by using the fitting means, attain to their desired end.

CHAPTER XIII.

MAN'S LAST END CANNOT BE ATTAINED IN THIS PRESENT LIFE.

If we give serious consideration to what has been said, we shall see how difficult, nay impossible, it would be for man to attain to his last end during the course of the present life. For, although it be true that beatitude is the last perfection of man, it is not every degree of contemplation of Divine things which can render a man happy. Although the contemplation of God forms the happiness of man, this contemplation must be perfect, with the fullest perfection of which human nature is capable. Whereas, during this mortal life, very few, scarce any one indeed, can attain to this perfection. Perfect contemplation demands a fullness of knowledge to which the greater part of mankind can never arrive. Some men are hindered there from by physical ineptitude, or by some imperfection in those interior senses which are the instruments used by the soul in the pursuit of knowledge. Others again, are so obtuse, that they can scarcely understand the clearest matters; whilst others are unable to devote themselves to contemplation, by reason of the duties imposed on them, through family cares, and the necessities of social life. And even those who are able to free themselves from these trammels, must serve a long apprenticeship before they can attain to the perfection of knowledge and contemplation. This for two reasons. Firstly, remembering that we attain to knowledge of immaterial things by means of sensible things, it is only reasonable to expect that an extensive knowledge of material things should be required before we can hope to attain to a perfect knowledge of such as are in the highest degree spiritual. Secondly, in order to attain to perfect contemplation, purity of heart, quiescence of the passions, and the possession of moral virtues, are essential; and these things are rarely met with except among the aged, and even among them are not possessed save by such as have laboured diligently for their acquisition. The greater number of those living in the world, being still young, and, but few of them having opportunity to devote themselves to the contemplation of the Truth, it follows that but a small number will be able to attain to perfect happiness in this life.

Neither need we be astonished at the fact, that it is exceptional to find souls capable of contemplation, when daily experience convinces us of the limitations of human understanding, and of the ease with which men are deceived in purely natural matters. How much more easily may we be deceived in things which are Divine? All our knowledge of natural things springs from the senses, and what more fallible than the eye, which tells us that the sun is a tiny sphere, whereas it is much larger than our entire earth? Again, the imagination can so obscure the intellect, as to render it difficult for us to believe that any beings exist, save such as are corporeal. Our understanding, again, often deceives us, persuading us to give credence to false and sophistical reasoning, as is proved by the many varying opinions even amongst clever men. The divers passions and affections of our soul, and our evil habits, are a further obstacle to our apprehension of the truth. If, then, our intellect be so shackled in its investigation of purely natural things, how much greater difficulty shall we not have in learning such as are Divine? The more we consider the hindrances which beset us in the acquisition of knowledge, the more clear it becomes that, if true happiness is only to be found in this life, very few amongst us can attain to it. Children, youths, women, and all such as are not capable of learning, and are occupied in human affairs, must be excluded from the chance of acquiring knowledge, and of attaining, through knowledge, to beatitude. Such an idea as this is, of course, absurd, since beatitude is the end of human life, and that for which all mankind is created.

But there is another reason which makes it impossible for man to be wholly happy in this life. This reason is, that happiness being the ultimate good of man, cannot be marred by any admixture of evil, and, being an all-sufficing good, it brings with it all other good; so that when perfect happiness is attained, nothing further remains for man to desire. But where shall we find, in this life, a man who wishes for nothing, and who, having a nature subject, as is our nature, to so many infirmities, enjoys, nevertheless, perfect immunity from every evil? Daily experience shows us, that even those who, like Priam, have been reputed happy, were beset by many misfortunes.

But let us assume that someone has, so far as it be possible in this mortal life, attained to the perfect contemplation of Divine things, and enjoys every other good, still even he cannot be called truly happy. For, since happiness means perfect tranquility of the human heart, and since all men have a natural, an unceasing desire to know, this desire must be an obstacle to perfect repose, as long as knowledge be not complete. The number of things in the world which men do not know, and yet desire to know, is almost infinite. Philosophers, after lifelong study, and much learning, have died leaving much unknown. For the things of which we have knowledge form but a small portion of that which there is to know, and our actual knowledge is most imperfect.

If, then, our intellect be so limited regarding natural things, how can we expect to understand such as are supernatural and Divine? The human heart cannot be satisfied with slight knowledge, but always desires more perfect knowledge. Thus it is, that the more it knows God, the more perfectly it desires to know Him; for natural impetus is swifter, as it nears the end, than at the beginning. Hence, it follows that, as we cannot, in the present life, attain to any perfect knowledge of God, neither can we enjoy perfect happiness.

But, supposing, for argument's sake, that a man should attain, in this world, to full knowledge of all things natural and Divine, he would still fail to be perfectly happy; because perfect knowledge cannot be acquired save in old age, when death draws nigh. Even if this knowledge could be gained in youth, it would still be no safeguard against death. The desire for immortality innate in all men; hence, all men desire to continue their lives, either in their children, or by some excellent work; for a wise man who loves a perfect life cannot fail to hate what destroys it. Therefore, were there no other life than this, the wisest man, yea, he whom we assume to be truly happy, could not fail to be saddened at the thought of death. A philosopher would not indeed banish the thought of death, for that would be the act of an unreasonable man; but neither can he be called happy, who has laboured all his life to acquire some good which he is unable to retain, and who knows not whether his end is to be in bliss, or in misery.

We see then, by the foregoing arguments, that, if there be no life beyond the grave, the lot of man is beyond measure wretched. For all other things are led by nature, and easily attain their end; but man is surrounded by difficulties, and either fails to find his end, or, if after much toil, he succeeds in finding it, he will be unable to retain it. That such should be the fate of the noblest of God's creatures on earth must appear, even to the most unlearned mind, an absurdity.

CHAPTER XIV.

THE SOUL OF MAN IS IMMORTAL.

The arguments set forth in the last chapter leave no
room to doubt that there is another life; and that the
human soul is immortal. For, as the Providence of
God conducts everything to its own end, man, if his
end be not attainable in this life, must be rendered
capable of securing it in a life to come. Were it otherwise, the Providence of GOD would not extend to human
affairs.

There is every proof of the existence of a germ of
immortality in the human soul. The operations of the
intellect cannot proceed from a physical force; because
they extend beyond corporeal things, and are occupied
with God. This argument has compelled philosophers
to acknowledge the immortality and immateriality of the
soul. It is, nevertheless, so difficult to understand how an
immaterial substance can be the form of the body, that
many different opinions have been held about the mode of
this immortality in man, which is called intellect. It cannot,
however, reasonably be denied, that the intellectual soul is
the form of the human body, since all men acknowledge
that it is the rationality of man which distinguishes him
from other animals. This distinction could not exist
were not a rational soul the form of man; for all specific
differences arise from form.

Again, it is universally allowed, that the peculiar
and pre-eminent activity of man is understanding and
reasoning; and man is the principle of this activity.

Man is composed of matter and form. We cannot say

that he is the principle of this activity by virtue of the matter of which he is composed, but solely by virtue of the form. Consequently, as this form is nothing but the intelligent soul, it is the intelligent soul which is the form of man.

Another argument for the immortality of the soul lies in the fact that man, like other animals, has the power of self-motion. Now, as the other animals move by means of their form, which is their soul, it follows that it must also be his soul which enables man to move. We know that man is governed by will and understanding. The form of man, therefore, must be an intelligent soul, capable of volition.

If a rational soul were not the form of man, the fact that a child, unable to use his understanding, is man would be inexplicable; neither could we see how intelligence could be attributed to a man who does not use his reason. If rational substance be not the form of man, but be self-subsisting, it will not be man, but that rational substance, which works with the intellect. We may, of course, maintain, with Plato that man is not composed of soul and body; but that he is merely soul which is united to the body as a motor is joined to that which is movable. But this opinion, if we adopt it, will lead us into many inconsistencies.

For, firstly, if the soul be the whole of man, to the exclusion of the body, man will not be sensitive; and when the soul leaves the body, corruption will not ensue; for the substance of a movable being does not change when the motor leaves it. It follows, likewise, that the human body does not live by the intellectual soul, and is not generated by union with the soul; for a movable thing is not generated by union with its motor. Human generation must, therefore, cease; for as, according to Plato, the soul is not generated, if the body be not man, one man will not be able to generate another. If neither the generated body, nor the soul and body together, but only the soul (which is not generated), be man, there will no longer, in human generation, be either fathers or children. These, and similar absurdities, beset those who will not acknowledge that the form of the body is an intelligent and immortal soul.

As the soul is, by its perfection, supreme among all natural and material forms , it partakes of the nature of incorporeal and immaterial substances; and, inasmuch as it partakes of the nature of inferior forms, it is said to be the form of the human body. In the perfection wherein it pertains to immaterial forms, it is separated from the body, so that the intellectual faculty of the soul is not, like its sensitive faculties, joined to any corporeal organ. Hence, the soul is sometimes called the nexus of the world, being the link between the highest and the lowest things.

We cannot then escape the conclusion, that the form of the body is a rational soul, which, in spite of the corruptibility of the body, remains incorruptible. This attribute of incorruptibility is proper to all intellectual substances, and is so for divers reasons: —

First , because every; perfection, must be proportioned to the thing of which it is the perfection, and, as universal and incorruptible things, and principally God, are the perfection of the intellectual soul, whose beatitude consists in contemplating them, the soul must be incorruptible.

Secondly, as we know that the perfection of the soul is proportionate to its abstraction from material, and its elevation to immaterial and Divine things, it is folly to say that the soul becomes corrupted by segregation from the body. Such an assertion is tantamount to saying, that separation from corporeal things is, at one and the same time, both the perfection, and the destruction of the soul. And it is equally futile to argue, that the soul attains perfection, by abstraction from the body, by means of the understanding", but suffers corruption by separation from the body by means of its essence. For operation follows nature; and therefore it is impossible that when the operation becomes perfect, the nature should become imperfect. Hence, it is quite unreasonable to say, that the intellectual soul suffers corruption when it is separated from the body.

The natural bias of mankind is a further argument in favor of the doctrine of the immortality of the soul. We see that all men are anxious about what takes place after death, and that none have been able to persuade themselves, that there is no future life. Thus the desire to know something of the hereafter is apparent in the writings of philosophers, of poets, and of orators. The fact of such a desire is a proof of our immortality; for if there were no future life, not only would this yearning for knowledge about it be of no service to man, but it would be injurious to him, by raising desires doomed only to disappointment. But if we assume that the intellectual soul is immortal, this natural desire to understand something of its future life is, far from being useless, both wholesome and necessary; it enables man to direct his thoughts to another life, and to tend towards beatitude.

It is evident, then, that if we deny that the intellectual soul is the form of the body, and is immortal, we shall be involved in many inconsistencies. We shall find it impossible to understand how man can be a rational animal endowed with free will, and justly liable to punishment for sin. Neither shall we be able to comprehend what is the End of man, and what the Providence of God in his regard. But, granted that an intellectual and immortal soul be the form of man, all these difficulties will disappear.

Since the consideration of the other life, which awaits the soul after death, exceeds the limits of human reason, we will here conclude our First Book, in order to treat in the next of the supernatural truths of Faith. For where reason halts, Faith begins. When we shall have shown, as we hope to do in the following Book, the truth of our faith, the immortality of the soul will be beyond doubt.

BOOK II.

METHOD OBSERVED THROUGHOUT THIS BOOK.

In our last Book we treated of those things which human reason is capable of grasping. It is our intention to discuss, in this book, those things which exceed reason, and to prove the truth of the Faith, both by natural means, and by the supernatural deeds of Christ. Since present occurrences carry more weight than past events, our first argument shall be founded on the deeds of Christians within the Church. We speak not of bad Christians, who are cut off from the body of Christ, but of such as are Christians in deed, as well as in name. We will next examine the works which Christ wrought in times past, and which are known to all the world. And, since He Himself by His words," I am come that they may have life, and may have it more abundantly" (John 10:10), shows that His chief work is to the perfection of Christian life, we will demonstrate the truth of the Faith of Christ : first, by arguments founded on the Christian life; secondly by others based on the cause of this life; and thirdly, by those drawn from the effects of this life. This chain of reasoning will embrace almost everything which is at present taking place within the Church militant.

CHAPTER I.

SOME TRUE RELIGION EXISTS IN THE WORLD.

In order to connect what has already been laid down with what still remains to be said, it is necessary to acknowledge the existence on earth of some true religion, or form of Divine worship. Religion, or worship, signifies the due honour paid to God, as to the universal Principle, Ruler, and End of all things. Every effect turns naturally to its cause; submits itself to its cause, in order to become like to it; and, in a certain sense, invokes the protection of its cause. By acting thus, the effect is paying honour and worship to its cause. Now, as man, is the effect of God, there must be in his nature an instinct prompting him to turn to God, to become subject to Him, to resemble Him, and to invoke Him, in order from Him to obtain beatitude. As no natural inclination is given us in vain, these promptings must spring from religion; and they are proofs that some true form of Divine worship exists in the world.

This fact is, again, proved on another count. Man is possessed of reason and of free will. Now, as reason is fallible on many points, especially in Divine matters, it follows that, if God had not revealed some true form of worship, we should have gone astray, as did the heathen before the advent of Christ, and should never have attained beatitude. Thus, our natural instinct would have misled us, and the Providence of God would have failed us, in a matter most closely pertaining to our salvation.

It is clear that a natural tendency to religion innate in the heart of man, from the fact that some form, though frequently an erroneous form, of Divine worship has existed through all generations. If, then, there be no possibility of satisfying this natural inclination, God has provided better for the needs of irrational creatures than for those of man.

It is the property of a cause to infuse its goodness and perfection into its effect, in order that this effect may, as far as is possible, resemble the cause. God, who is the Supreme Good and the First Cause of all things, desires, more earnestly than does any other cause, to infuse His goodness into man in order to bring him to beatitude; and, as the perfection of man consists in that interior homage whereby he subjects himself to God, it is clear, that God cannot have made this interior homage impossible, and that, in other words, some true religion exists in the world.

CHAPTER II.

RELIGION IS BOTH INTERIOR AND EXTERIOR.

God can be honoured by man, both in body and in spirit; and, therefore, religion must be both interior and exterior. Interior worship is paid to God by means of the understanding and the will; and exterior homage by means of ceremonies and sacrifices.

Interior religion, then, strictly speaking, signifies uprightness of heart before God, and perfection of life. For, as every effect honours its cause chiefly by its perfection, man cannot pay to God a greater homage than that of a perfect life. This, therefore, constitutes the truth and completeness of Divine worship, even as the perfection of a work gives glory to the worker.

And, as we pay homage to God, not only in order to honour Him, but also in order to receive beatitude from Him; and as a good life is a more sure way of attaining to beatitude than are sacrifices and ceremonies, it is evident that perfection of life is a more true religion than any exterior form of worship. God is not a body, but Pure Act: therefore man renders to Him more perfect worship by purity of heart, than by external actions, for "God is a Spirit, and they that adore Him, must adore Him in spirit and in truth" (John 4:24).

CHAPTER III.

NO BETTER LIFE CAN BE FOUND THAN THE CHRISTIAN
LIFE.

As true religion consists in the perfection of human life;
and as no better life than the Christian life can be conceived, it follows that there can be no better religion than
the Christian religion. This assertion is easily proved.
Animal life is more perfect than vegetative life; and among
the different degrees of animal life, that one is the highest
which is the most largely endowed with
sensible feeling. If, further, it be the case that intellectual
cognition be superior to sensible feeling, it is certain that
the life of man is more perfect than that of animals.
Among men are likewise found degrees, not of life but
of perfection; for, as man is rational, those men are the
most perfect who live the most nearly according to
reason; for he who lives not according to reason resembles a beast rather than a man. Again, among those
who live according to reason, there are divers degrees of
perfection. For, as the end of the life of reason is the
contemplation of Divine things, so the more perfectly
a man abstract himself from earthly things, and devotes
himself to the contemplation of that which is Divine, the
more perfect will be his life. Since the Christian life
consists in separating ourselves, not only from temporal
things, but also from self-love, and in drawing, by love
and contemplation, near to God, so as to become like to
Him, and, so far as possible, to be made one with Him,
it is clear that nothing better than the Christian life can
exist.

As we have already said, the more, perfectly a man

follows the dictates of reason, the more perfect will be his life. It is evident, therefore, that the Christian life does nothing and permits nothing, not even the least thing, which is contrary to reason; but that it submits in all things to the Divine Law.

A virtuous life tends to the contemplation of heavenly things, and finds its end in this contemplation. Great purity of heart is requisite for the attainment of this end. Consequently, as no life so purifies us, and renders us so apt for contemplation, as does the Christian life, it follows, that nothing better can be found on earth than Christianity.

CHAPTER IV.

THE END PRESENTED TO US BY THE CHRISTIAN RELIGION IS THE BEST WHICH CAN POSSIBLY BE CONCEIVED.

In order to show that there can be no life better than the Christian life, we shall first prove that the end set in view by the Christian religion is the best possible end, and the one most in accordance with reason, and that the means furnished by Christianity for the attainment of that end are those best adapted to that purpose. It is self-evident that the end held out to us by the Christian religion is the best possible en d, seeing that it is God, and the vision and fruition of God; and this vision and fruition is not such as may be gained by means of creatures, but that wherein God is beheld "face to face". Many reasons can be adduced to prove that this clear vision of God is the end of our human life. First, as we have already proved, man's beatitude cannot be attained in this life; therefore, if he be not created in vain, it must be "attainable in the next. But if, in the next life, his happiness were to consist in knowing and contemplating God by means of creatures, it would not be complete happiness, for his heart would not be at rest; and happiness consists in the quiescence or satisfaction of all desires. This tranquility would be incomplete, whether his knowledge of creatures were perfect or imperfect. If he knew creatures imperfectly, his heart would not be at rest, because he would desire that this knowledge should be perfect. For we know, by daily experience, that we desire distinct and particular cognition of the things which we know only in a general and confused manner. Were his knowledge of creatures perfect, he would still desire to know that on which they depend. For it is natural to us when we see an effect to wish to know its cause; and the more perfectly we know the effect the more intensely do we wish to know its cause, just as the heavier an object is, with the greater energy does it gravitate to its centre. Hence, as man becomes happier and more perfect in proportion to his knowledge of Divine things; and, as his desire of this knowledge increases proportionately to his progress therein, it is certain that his wish for this knowledge will never cease until he attains his Last End. This End can be naught but God. For, as we know by experience, our hearts can never be satisfied by any

finite thing. Our intellect is superior to everything finite because there is nothing superior to its capacity; and our ability to understand increases in proportion to our knowledge. Hence, as everything which is inferior to God is finite; and, as our intellect is capable of knowing infinite things, it is true to say that no creature can fill even one-tenth part of our heart. It becomes, therefore, not merely reasonable, but even necessary, to acknowledge that the happiness of man consists in the vision of God, who alone is greater than the human heart.

Every natural movement, as all philosophers will admit, tends to some end, in which, when it is attained, the thing which is moved finds rest. Now God, who is the term of human desire, is the satisfaction of the human heart, leaving naught else to be desired. And this because everything else, being finite, will bear no comparison to Him who is infinite; and, also, because all perfection of creatures is to be found in its fullest excellence in Him who is their Cause. Thus, when the soul of man possesses God it possesses all things; for the intellect which knows Him, will know creatures far more perfectly; and, although the excessive intensity of things sensible weakens the sense perceiving them, the excess of that which is intelligible, far from injuring the understanding, perfects it.

But we must remember that, as God is infinite, and is outside the realm of creation, our intellect cannot, by virtue of its natural light, attain to the vision of Him; because nothing can act beyond the limits of its nature. Nevertheless, our understanding, which is capable of rising to infinite things, may, by the Divine Power, be enabled to behold that which is naturally invisible to it. Thus the beatitude of man consists in the vision of God, and he is enabled to enjoy it by means of a supernatural light, which is called "the light of glory". It is plain then, that no more reasonable or better end could be devised, as the term of human life, than the end set before us by the Christian religion.

CHAPTER V.

A CHRISTIAN LIFE IS THE BEST POSSIBLE MEANS FOR ATTAINING TO HAPPINESS.

If the vision of God be the end of human life, God, who has made nothing in vain, must have given us some means of attaining to it. For, just as it would be useless for us to possess the power of motion, had we not limbs wherewith to move, so would it be futile to be created for an end, if we have no means of reaching it. The Christian religion teaches, that the means whereby we are to attain to the vision of God are, purity of heart, and ^race, together with all the virtues supernaturally infused into the soul.

We shall see how true and how reasonable this doctrine is, if we remember that a means must be proportioned to its end. Now, as the end of man is the supernatural vision of God, the Supreme Object of intelligence, there is needed, in order to attain to it, perfect purity of heart, consisting in a complete "aversion of the mind and heart from the love of corporeal things, together with a con- version to things incorporeal and Divine. This purity of heart is far more explicitly enjoined by the Christian religion than by any philosopher. Christianity has included all that philosophy has taught on the subject; at the same time defining more clearly what is meant by this purity of heart, and showing that mere natural virtue, such as is inculcated by philosophers, is not sufficient for the attainment of an end infinitely superior to nature. Christianity teaches that the purity of heart which springs from temperament, imagination, natural religion, from the influence of the heavenly bodies, or from any other created thing, will not suffice to bring us to the vision of God, Our purity must be the fruit of Divine grace. A fuller explanation of the subject may be found in the treatise on The Simplicity of Christian Life, 18 in which it is shown that purity of heart, and the perfect Christian life, is not the result of natural love, nor is it the creation of the imagination nor even of reason; that it is not influenced by the heavenly bodies nor by any spiritual creatures; but that it comes from the grace of God, supernaturally infused into the soul. We need not repeat all that is written in that book, about the most perfect means for attaining the perfection of the Christian life. Suffice it to say, that the life of a true Christian, which embraces the highest form of a holy life, both natural and supernatural, is most conducive to perfect happiness.

CHAPTER VI.

THE CHRISTIAN LIFE IS A MOST SURE MEANS OF ATTAINING TO BEATITUDE.

If, as has been proved, there be in the world some true religion, consisting mainly in uprightness of life; and if the Christian religion surpasses every other; we must acknowledge Christianity to be true, not only in its interior spirit, but also in its exterior forms. For there must be some true external worship which corresponds, in all things, with interior religion. Therefore, if Christians live according to the teaching of their Faith, paying due homage to God, both in order to honour Him and to attain to beatitude, we cannot doubt that they will thus arrive at their Last End.

If, again, it pertains to Divine Providence to bring things to their End by fitting means, and if there are no better means than the Christian religion whereby man may attain to beatitude, who can doubt that the Christian religion conducts man to the eternal enjoyment of the beatific vision?

Further, if God be just — and we must confess that He is; and if He exercise Providence over human things, He will not suffer those who have obeyed His command ments and professed the Christian religion to fail in the attainment of their end. He must bring either some men to beatitude, or none. If none are to attain to beatitude, creation is in vain. Some men therefore, must be saved, and among them God will not pass over true Christians, who are of all men the best fitted and prepared for beatitude. If Christians do not attain to the fruition of their End, we must needs confess that none others can hope to do so; that all we have hitherto taught and proved is false; and that all men are living in disorder and confusion. For where there is no last end there can be no order in life. It would follow likewise, that man lives by chance, more miserably than the animals.

This would only be one of many similar absurdities which would inevitably follow, were we to deny the value of Christianity.

It must be acknowledged, then, that the teaching of the Christian religion about the end of man, and the means necessary for its attainment, is most reasonable; and we must confess this religion to be true.

CHAPTER VII.

THE FAITH OF CHRIST IS TRUE, BECAUSE IT CAUSES MEN TO LEAD A PERFECT LIFE.

In proving Christianity to be true, we have hitherto made use of arguments founded on the good life of true Christians. We will now proceed to examine the causes of this virtuous life. One of the chief causes is, as the Scripture teaches, the belief in Christ informed by charity :"The justice of God, by faith of Jesus Christ, unto all, and upon all them that believe in Him" (Rom. 3:22)."Without faith it is impossible to please God" (Heb. 11:6). By faith informed by charity, we mean that, loving Christ crucified above all things, we believe Him to be truly God and truly Man, One with the Father and the Holy Ghost, and distinct from them only in Person.

Universal experience demonstrates the truth of what we say. For in the present day it is evident to all, and still more was it so in days gone by, that, as soon as a man grasps the Faith of Christ and becomes inflamed with His love, he begins to lead a Christian life, and makes progress in perfection, in proportion to his in- crease of faith and charity; and at the same time he is confirmed in those virtues, in proportion to his advance in perfection. On the other hand, they who lead bad lives are deficient in faith; and they that lack faith "lead bad lives. As this is a truth admitting no denial, we will investigate it, and, by inquiring into the causes of such wonderful effects, will deduce proofs of the truth of the Christian religion.

First. Since all perfection depends upon its cause, no effect can be more perfect than its cause. Therefore, if all the truth and uprightness of the Christian life depends upon the Faith of Christ, as upon its cause, it is impossible that the Faith of Christ should not be true. And if this faith be true, we must, with Christians, confess that Christ is God, and that His religion is the true religion revealed by God.

Again. It is impossible that falsehood and evil should be the cause of truth and goodness; for evil, in so far as it is evil, and falsehood, in so far as it is falsehood, are nothingness. If, then, the Faith of Christ were false, His love would be vain and evil. Now, a life so perfect as is the Christian life could not spring from falsehood and iniquity. Therefore, the Christian religion must be true.

Furthermore. If this religion be untrue it is the most stupid falsehood that can possibly be conceived; for to say (were it not true) that a crucified man is God would be the extreme of folly. Now, as the Christian life is a perfect life, it cannot spring from untruth; for all rightly ordered life proceeds from correctness of understanding, and all error in human conduct springs from some mistake on the part of the intellect.

It must also be remembered that capacity for improvement in any nature is proportioned to the good disposition already existing therein. Now, as the perfection of our intellect is truth, and as purity of heart is the disposition which enables him to become steadfast in truth, the more a man is purged from earthly affections the better he will know the truth, the more closely he will embrace it, and the further he will banish falsehood from his soul. If this be true, surely Christians, since their lives are purer than those of other men, would be the first to know if their religion were false. We see, however, that far from rejecting their faith, Christians cling more closely to it in proportion as they increase in perfection, and that their increase in perfection is pro- portioned to their steadfastness in their faith. Therefore, their faith cannot be false.

Again, as God is the First Cause moving all things, both spiritual and corporal, it is certain that it is He who must move the human understanding, and that, apart from Him, no truth can be known. But who can doubt that God will inspire to know the truth those who are prepared for its reception, rather than those who are not thus disposed, and especially when the truth concerns eternal salvation? Since then true Christians are better prepared than are any other men to embrace the truth, we cannot doubt that, if the Faith of Christ were false, they would be enlightened by God to reject it. To think otherwise, would be to doubt the providence and goodness of God.

The end regulates the means used to attain it, and he that errs as to his end, will err also as to the means which he uses. Christians do not err as to the means which they adopt for attaining to beatitude, and therefore they do not err as to their end. Now, as all Christians profess that Christ is their End, and that they strive to be made like to Him in this life in order to enjoy Him in the next, it cannot be erroneous to teach that Christ is God, and is the End of human life.

Again, God proceeds in all things in a certain order, and in His wisdom governs inferior things by those that are superior to them. And since the cause is always more perfect than the effect, He has ordained noblest causes for the noblest effects. As there is not in the world a more noble effect than the Christian life, it follows that the cause from which it springs must be the noblest possible. Since the Christian life is an effect of the Faith of Christ, we must acknowledge that Faith, far from being a fable, is the noble cause of a noble effect.

All secondary causes are instruments of a primary-cause. Therefore Christ, the Man who was crucified, is the instrument whereby God chooses to produce that wonderful effect — the Christian life. Had Christ, in spite of His assertions, not been God, His pride and mendacity would have been unparalleled; and God would have used a bad instrument to produce a most perfect effect — a course quite out of keeping with His wisdom.

The more closely an effect resembles its cause, the more perfect does it become. We become more holy and more Divine in proportion as we walk in the footsteps of Christ and become like to Him, This is a clear proof that Christ is true God, and the Cause of man.

Causes are known by their effects, and one of the best arguments in favour of the Christian religion is the reflection that, whereas heathen philosophers have laboured for years to establish rules of conduct, they have gained but few disciples, of whom even the most virtuous have never attained to that standard of living which has been so quickly reached by innumerable Christians of both sexes and of every race and condition. No one who reflects on this fact can fail to see that there is no comparison between the efficacy of the heathen philosophy and of the Christian Faith, which is able to render the proud, avaricious, and luxurious, humble, benevolent and chaste. Everyone, consequently, must acknowledge that Christ, as God, is the

Principal Cause of human perfection, and, "as Man, is its Means and Instrumental Cause.

CHAPTER VIII.

THE DOCTRINES TAUGHT BY CHRISTIANITY ARE TRUE, AND COME FROM GOD.

The reading, hearing, and study of Holy Scripture is both a cause of our Christian life, and the substance and foundation of our religion, of which the object is the truth of the Faith. Having examined the arguments founded on the Faith of Christ, we now proceed to investigate those drawn from Holy Writ.

We know that there can be no certain truth or knowledge about future things which may or may not happen. Even philosophers, who were truly wise, admitted this. These can be known to God alone, and to man only when God reveals them to him. Man could not know them, unless it pleased God to make them known. Now Holy Scripture, in almost every portion, but especially in the Old Testament, has foretold things which should come to pass, and which depended on man's free will. These prophecies concern not only general, but also particular things; and they relate to events which were to occur, not only in one year or in ten, but in a hundred or a thousand, or three or four thousand years; they were to happen not only to the Jews and to Christ and His Church, but were to concern also the Assyrians, the Chaldeans, the Persians, the Medes, the Greeks, the Romans, and other lesser kingdoms. 19 Now many of the events foretold by the Prophets have come to pass; and the fact of their fulfillment inspires us with confidence that any that have not yet been accomplished will eventually be verified. We must, therefore, acknowledge the Holy Scriptures to be, not a work of human ingenuity, but the revelation of God's Providence towards us.

God alone has prescience of the future. Therefore, no man, be he ever so diligent or wise, can order the wars and doings of kings and princes, and the names and places, and divers actions and circumstances of men in such a way that they shall foreshadow things to come. The reason is simple. God has the ordering of things which are to come; they are subject to Him. They are beyond the power and knowledge of man. The Old Testament foretells the New Testament, and the things which Christ has done and suffered, both in His Person and in His Church. Therefore, we have good reason to believe that both the Old Testament and the New are the Word of God.

It is not reasonable to say that Christians have interpreted the prophecies of Scripture according to their desires. For, taking into account the differences of times and circumstances, of language and of authors, the extraordinary uniformity which exists between the Old and the New Testaments would not be possible, were they not the work of one Mind, which knows all that has taken place at all times. Neither can this uniformity be ascribed to chance, since there is no discord or want of harmony between the two Testaments, but perfect agreement between them, even in the smallest particulars; so that what is obscure in one passage is explained in another; and the Scripture interprets itself. Although those who have not studied the Bible may be ignorant of this fact, the truth of what I say will be acknowledged by all who examine Holy Scripture with faith, humility and purity of heart.

It is on account of this harmony between the Old and New Testaments, that the Bible possesses the dignity of an allegorical meaning. But, observe, that by an allegorical, we do not mean a fabulous, interpretation — such as we find in the poets — for we interpret parables also, and their interpretation is not called an allegorical, but literal and parabolic meaning. We do not intend by the words of the fable or parable to express what is signified by the words themselves, but rather what we understand by the meaning underlying those words. An allegory requires, first, that the words should narrate, not a fiction, but some fact that has really occurred; secondly, that this fact should prefigure some future event; thirdly, that the fact narrated should have taken place not only on account of its intrinsic importance, but also as a forecast of some future occurrence. As no one but God can compose such allegories, and as the Holy Scriptures are full of them, it is clear that only God can be their Author."

The language and style of the Bible are so peculiar, that none of our most learned and eloquent Doctors have ever been able to imitate it; nor has it been copied by any other writer. The Prophets, although they lived at different times and wrote with varying degrees of elegance, have all retained the same mode of expression, which has not been imitated by any other author, and is, in fact, inimitable. This is a clear proof that the Holy Scriptures are a Divine and not a human work.

A further confirmation of what we say may be perceived, if we observe the effects which proceed from the Scriptures; for the virtue of a cause is known by its effect. Now, as upon earth there is no more sublime effect than the Christian life, and as the Bible is a most powerful instrumental cause and foundation of this life, it is manifest that it can only proceed from the First Cause of the Christian life, via., God. Long experience teaches us that human science avails but little in the formation of virtuous habits; for, before Christianity-was preached, the whole world was wrapped in the darkness of ignorance and sin; but from the time the Apostles taught the truth, mankind has been enlightened and initiated into many heavenly secrets.

And even in our own days, we see how the teaching of the Holy Scripture has more efficacy than has any other doctrine, in enlightening and consoling: men, and in inclining them to live virtuously. For the preachers who discourse only on philosophical subjects, and pay great attention to oratorical effect, produce scarcely any fruit among their Christian hearers. Whereas our fore-fathers, who in past times confined themselves to the simple preaching of the Holy Scriptures, were able to fill their hearers with Divine love, enabling them to rejoice in affliction and even in martyrdom. I speak also from personal experience. For, when at one time (in order to demonstrate the profundity of Holy Scripture to sciolists, proud of their intelligence) I was wont to discourse on subtle points of philosophy, I found that the people who heard me were inattentive. But as soon as I devoted myself to the exposition of the Bible, I beheld all eyes riveted upon me, and my audience so intent upon my words, that they might have been carved out of stone. I found, likewise, that when I set aside theological questions, and confined myself to explaining Holy Scripture, my hearers received much more light, and my preaching bore more fruit, in the conversion of men to Christ and to a perfect life. For Holy Scripture contains that marvelous doctrine, which, more surely than a two-edged sword pierces men's hearts with love, which has adorned the world with virtue, and has over thrown idolatry, superstition, and numberless errors. This proves that it can proceed from none but God.

The more completely the human intellect is purified, the more capable it becomes of apprehending the truth. Now, as there is no purity of life so perfect as that produced by Christianity, Christian doctors, of whom there are many, would (were the Bible not the work of God) on account of their learning and their holiness, be the first to discern the fact. So far, however, from denying the Divine inspiration of the Scriptures, the Fathers of the Church have left many volumes extolling the teaching of Holy Writ, and have written and preached that it is unlawful to alter one iota of the sacred text. Some of them have, in defense of the Divine origin of the Bible, even shed their blood. If these men had not had some certainty that the Scriptures were the work of God, they would, most assuredly, not have sacrificed their lives in such a cause.

Again, truth can never disagree with truth; truth must be in harmony with truth; but it is invariably at war with falsehood. Now, as every science agrees with Holy Scripture, it is evident that it must contain, not falsehood, but truth. The leaders of thought, in every branch of science, have proved that no true science is repugnant to Holy Scripture. Therefore, Christians are not forbidden to study any science, save divination and such like pernicious superstitions, which are derided by all true scientists. This harmony between science and the Bible is a proof of the truth of the latter. Were the Scriptures false, they would infallibly contradict science; whereas the Doctors of the Church show that the Bible and science agree; and they are able to explain any apparent discrepancy between them.

Further. The more truth is impugned, the more, if it have a defender, it becomes clear to the human intellect, which has a natural tendency to truth as to its own perfection. Christianity has been always opposed, both by philosophers and by temporal sovereigns, and has invariably proved itself invincible. This, again, is a strong proof of its truth; for, had it been false, it must, inevitably, have succumbed to persecution.

CHAPTER IX.

THE TRUTH OF THE FAITH PROVED BY ARGUMENTS FOUNDED ON THE PRAYER AND CONTEMPLATION OF CHRISTIANS.

Faith, and meditation on the Holy Scriptures are not only the cause, but also the nourishment and perfection, of the Christian life. Experience, both past and present, shows that Christians given to continual prayer, acquire great perfection in a short space of time, and find such delight in spiritual things, that everything else seems worthless to them. This is the case not with a few learned men only, but with many also of the uneducated. In fact, this is the experience of all, both men and women of every degree, who exercise themselves in prayer. On this fact we intend to found an argument for the truth of our faith.

First. Since God is Pure Act, Supreme Truth, and' Infinite Light, it follows that the nearer man approaches to Him (in spirit not in body), the more he will partake of the Divine purity, truth and light. Now, as the Christian life is more pure and perfect than any other, it must be nearer to God than any other life; and Christians approach most closely to Him when they are engaged in the exercise of prayer and contemplation, which renders the soul peculiarly capable of receiving the Divine purity, truth, and light. Since, then, it is by prayer and contemplation, that Christians are confirmed in their Faith in Christ Crucified, and fired with love of Him, it is undeniable that the Faith is Divine truth and light.

Again. Our understanding is naturally inclined to delight in truth, to desire it, and to shun falsehood; and the more a natural inclination is purified, the more vehement it becomes. Prayer purifies the understanding more efficaciously than does any other mental act; and therefore, if in time of prayer, the soul be more drawn to embrace the Faith of Christ than at any other time, this is a proof that the Faith is truth and not falsehood.

Further. Christians, while they pray, make their supplications to God for the sake of Christ Crucified, and through His merits; and nevertheless they ask for great things. Even should this assertion be disbelieved, it cannot, at least, be denied that the chief prayer of a Christian is for grace to live a Christian life, and for joy and peace of soul. Now, if Christ were not the One whom they think Him to be, God would surely enlighten them to see the truth. Or, if they preferred to remain obstinately in error, their prayers would not be, as they now are, heard for the sake of Christ.

Again. No cause prevents matter from receiving a form; and no natural motor prevents a thing from tending to its end. As beatitude is the end to be attained by a good life and by prayer, and as man cannot move himself to pray and to live virtuously, but must be inspired thereto by God, who inspires Christians to so perfect a life, and to such sublimity of prayer, and confirms them in Faith, it is manifest that Faith is the mean by which we are to attain to beatitude, and that this Faith must proceed from God.

Every cause listens, if we may so speak, to the prayer of its effect, and by this prayer we mean the desire of the effect for its perfection, which, if its dispositions be ordered aright, it will seek to obtain from its cause. We see in the natural order, that when matter is duly prepared, the cause does not delay in giving it form; and this proceeds from the goodness of the cause, for the characteristic of good is to communicate itself Hence, as God is Supreme Goodness, He exceeds all causes in listening to the prayer of His effects, when they are disposed to receive His influx. Now, the Christian life, especially as exhibited in the act of prayer and contemplation, is the best possible preparation for being heard by God; and the prayers of Christians are, most surely, not made in vain. There is nothing which Christians more earnestly implore of God than to be enlightened as to the truth. Thus David, in the name of all, prays, saying, "Enlighten mine eyes, O Lord, that I may never sleep in death"(Ps. 12:4). And therefore we must believe that true Christians are enlightened as to the truth which pertains to salvation. The more they pray, the more confirmed do the y become in their faith in Christ. Thus, we have good grounds for believing this faith to be true, and not false.

A further argument is, that if Christ be not God, it would be blasphemy to believe and to confess that He is God — One with the Father and the Holy Ghost — and to pray through His merits. How could the Divine Goodness leave in such blindness Christians, the best of mankind, always ready to extirpate any error which may dishonor the Divine Majesty? It is absurd to say that God leaves them in their disbelief, because they obstinately persevere in it. For, were this the case, why should He hear their blasphemous prayers? Why, on the contrary, should He not punish them severely?

If, again, the Faith of Christ be false, could there be a more absurd superstition than to adore a crucified man as God? Our understanding naturally loves truth and abhors falsehood; how then could it be possible, that innumerable Christians, amongst them men of vast genius and great learning, could so delight in the contemplation and love of Christ Crucified, as for His sake, not only willingly to bear, but even eagerly to desire, hunger and thirst, labours, threats, opprobrium, scourges, imprisonment, and even death? Truly the finger of God is here.

CHAPTER X.

PROOFS OF THE TRUTH OF THE CHRISTIAN RELIGION FOUNDED ON ITS EXTERNAL FORMS OF WORSHIP.

Our arguments for the truth of Christianity have hitherto been drawn from the interior aspect of that religion. We will now proceed to proofs based on its Sacraments, ceremonies, and other external rites. We will, instead of considering them individually, which would be a lengthy task, group all the ceremonies and Sacraments of the Church under the one which is chief and most venerable, viz., the Sacrament of the Blessed Eucharist. We know by experience, and since the first days of Christianity it has been proved, that the reverent observance of this exterior worship is the cause, the nourishment, and the perfection of the Christian life; that they who frequent the Sacraments devoutly become more holy day by day; and that they who treat them with irreverent familiarity become more hardened than other men in sin. We see this fact exemplified in priests, who, day and night, administer the Sacraments, and perform the ceremonies of the Church. For, those who do so devoutly, are most holy men, so completely purified from earthly affection, and so closely united to God, that, for love of Him, they fear not to expose their lives.

Those, on the other hand, who perform their sacred duties irreligiously, are worse than any other men; for, besides being guilty of pride, avarice, envy, and other sins, they are in the most hopeless state possible, for they are incorrigible; and the admonitions, reprimands and good examples, which cause others to amend, are for them only an incitement to scorn, hatred, and worse sin. We cannot therefore deny that the same Sacraments produce contrary effects in different men. We must now investigate the cause of this phenomenon. It is in no wise repugnant to philosophy, that contrary effects should, by reason of contrary disposition of matter, spring from the same cause. For, we see how the rays of the sun harden the earth, and melt ice, cause a well- planted tree to bear flower and fruit, and wither another whose roots have not struck deeply. The two effects of which we have been speaking, viz., the good effect produced by the Sacrament's on good priests and religious, and 'the bad effect produced on those that are bad cannot spring from a false or empty cause. For, if the externals of religion did not depend on God, and were not the instruments of Divine virtue and truth, they could not produce an effect so excellent as to give birth to the Christian life, and to nourish and perfect it. For as this life is wholly spiritual and Divine, it cannot proceed from any physical power. Who is there that believes that baptism with water, anointing with chrism, smoke of incense, oblation of bread and wine upon the altar, and other rites and ceremonies of the same description, could of themselves, without any other power, suffice to render a soul perfect? Surely if these things were human inventions, or deceits of the devil, they could not produce holy lives.

But, perhaps you will say, the Christian life is not produced by this external worship, but by the exercise of virtues, and by the credulity of men, who, believing these exterior ceremonies to be Divine, do by means of them lead a good life, and thus make progress in virtue. Why is it, then, we would answer, that other men who practice virtue without the Sacraments, never attain to the same degree of holiness, as these good priests? Surely, if external worship were false and useless, those who ab- stained from it would become all the better, not being contaminated by error; and priests who despised these rites and ceremonies, and made a jest of them, would be the best of men. Daily experience, however, shows us, that facts are quite otherwise.

Again, it stands to reason that as God is the Supreme Truth, man, the more closely he draws nigh to God, partakes more fully of His light and truth; and the more he becomes involved in error and falsehood, the further he recedes from God. But we know that those who devoutly frequent the Sacraments, and make use of the ceremonies of the Church, become so united to God, that manifest signs of the presence of the Divine light appear in their countenance, and many are wrapped in ecstasy, and their faces are then so transfigured, that they appear to all men attractive and venerable. And although such phenomena were more common in past times than at present, these marvels are still often to be seen in our own days, amongst both men and women, learned and ignorant. Whence come these ecstasies, and this holy contemplation, this fervor of spirit, and these tears which accompany exterior worship? In truth, if these external ceremonies are not ordained by God, they are full of absurdities and fallacies; for they are all typical of things spiritual and Divine; and our churches, sacraments, altars, priestly vestments, sacred psalmody, and ceremonies all typify falsehoods, especially concerning Christ, of whom they are a figure, and they amount to nothing save useless lies. But if these exterior rites are a mere mockery, good men would not take such delight in them, nor by their means draw so near to God. For, as we have said, in proportion as men are involved in error, they recede from God. Hence, we must conclude that the ritual of the Church is full of grace and truth. The wonderful ceremonial of the Church, again, and the symbolical signification of her rites wherein there is nothing trivial, nothing irrational — but everything, even the most minute detail, is typical of some mystery — proves, that these rites are not a human invention, but a Divine ordinance. It is not our intention here to enlarge upon the meaning of the ecclesiastical ceremonies, as this subject will be briefly handled in the next Book.

If, however, any one wishes to know more of these mysteries without further delay, he will find them explained in the Christian doctrine; and he will see that there is no less harmony and order in the ceremonies of the Church than in the operations of nature. And, unless he be thoroughly perverse, he will be forced to acknowledge, that our worship is the outcome, not of a human, but of a Divine Spirit.

CHAPTER XI

THE TRUTH OF CHRISTIANITY EVIDENCED BY ITS EFFECTS ON THE INTERIOR LIFE OF CHRISTIANS.

We have, to the best of our poor ability, proved the truth of the Faith by arguments founded on the internal and external causes of the Christian life. We will next proceed to demonstrate its truth by its effects on this life. Its chief interior effect is peace and joy of spirit, and liberty of soul. We see this effect exemplified in the Saints of former times (when there was more fervor than at present). They enjoyed a serenity and, peace of mind which enabled them, not only to remain unshaken in the midst of affliction, but even to rejoice at martyrdom.

Now, as this joy in the midst of tribulation increases in them in proportion as they draw nearer to Christ, we see that peace of soul can only be attained by union with God^ the last end and only satisfaction of the human heart, in whom alone we can find rest. Those who are closely united to Him have such firm hope of enjoying happiness after this life, that they make no account of the good things of this world, and fear neither persecution nor loss of life, but eagerly look forward to death, as the passage to eternal bliss. And God, though He is everywhere, dwells specially in such souls as these, by His grace and love, and by the gift of contemplation. He sustains them by His presence, delivering them from all fear, and giving them such liberty of spirit, that they are neither cast down by adversity, nor uplifted by prosperity.

This peace, joy, and freedom of soul cannot proceed from any natural human power, weakened as we are by sensuality and ignorance. It must be a supernatural gift of God, causing us to lift our eyes to the Divine light and the beatitude promised to us.

We can prove that this peace of soul is caused by union with God, if we reason in the following manner. The soul is one, and all its powers spring from it. If, then, the soul be fixed on the operation of one power, it cannot attend to the operation of another; just as in intense contemplation the operations of the senses are suspended, and in great physical pain or enjoyment the understanding is no longer exercised. Hence, humanly speaking, it would be quite impossible that, in the midst of intense bodily torture, the intellect should enjoy peace and happiness. And, yet, we behold this phenomenon in innumerable martyrs, of both sexes, and of every rank of life. Of course the sages of this world will adduce examples of a few individuals, who, although not Christians, have experienced the same ecstasy in the midst of sufferings. But the Christians in whom this miracle has been wrought are innumerable, and the least child who is a true Christian is superior to all the heathen saints, whose erroneous judgment and perverted affections are conspicuous in their writings. Thus, this power of rejoicing in the midst of suffering, is not natural it is a supernatural gift of God. This again is a proof of the veracity of Christianity. For were the Faith of Christ (which is the cause of these wonderful effects), proved to be false, it would not come from God, and Christians would thus be left to their natural weakness, and involved in many errors.

The more virtuously a man lives, the more clearly he discerns the truth, and the better he loves good and hates evil and falsehood. If, then, the religion of Christ were not true, Christians would live in error, and their persistence in adoring Christ as God would be criminal. But experience shows us that Christians are confirmed in their faith, and enjoy peace, and joy, and liberty of soul in proportion to their virtue. This would certainly not be the case were Christianity a falsehood.

The truth of our Faith is also confirmed by the example of the many religious of both sexes, who in these days, as well as in past times, have from desire of perfection left friends and kinsfolk, riches, pleasure, and even their own will, and have retired into a cloister in some far-off land, where, submitting to strangers, they have promised to observe poverty, to possess nothing save with the permission of their superior, to preserve chastity of soul and body to fast and watch as much as their weakness will permit, and to practice obedience to all commands. Thus, they renounce worldly possessions, earthly happiness and their own will; and yet they live as joyfully, and take as much delight in praising God, as if they had all that earth can give. With one consent they acknowledge that all their peace and joy of soul is based on the Faith in Jesus Crucified. And we cannot repute them as fools, since among them are not only ignorant persons, but men renowned for learning, prudence, and judgment, who would, were their Faith false, speedily recognize their error. Hence, we must reckon that the cause of this wonderful effect is the religion of Christ, which is not false but true.

As these religious, being in a state of life wherein a high degree of perfection is attainable, make every effort to advance in perfection, it follows that they are more fitted than are other men to receive heavenly illumination. Were the faith false, it would not be possible for its false- hood to

be disguised during so many centuries, and among so many worthy men; nor could these men confirm their religion every hour in their hearts, by
their words, their works, and their innumerable writings; nor, being in the greatest subjection, live in such spiritual liberty and joy.

Again. Every cause does, as far as possible, direct its effect to its end, especially when the effect is disposed to receive the influx of its cause. Hence, God, being supremely good, conducts all things to their end, unless they are hindered, by their unfitness, from attaining to it.

Now, as no better disposition for attaining to beatitude can be found than the life of religious, it follows that they must be guided by God to beatitude, and that their peace and joy are a participation of beatitude. As this aptitude for beatitude springs from the Faith of Christ, and increases in proportion to the growth of that Faith, it is clear that the Faith cannot be false, or God would be fostering errors and spurious joy in the souls of well-disposed men, and would thus be leading them astray.

All joy again is based on love, which is that first act of the appetite and will, on which all other acts depend. Now, as the happiness of religious is not centered on worldly goods, which they have relinquished, and as they unanimously acknowledge that the well-spring of their joy is the Faith of Christ and the hope of another life, they cannot be living in error. For, the uprightness of their life would cause them to perceive their mistake; and thus would banish their peace of mind. But we see that they experience quite contrary effects, which prove that the Faith of Christ is true.

CHAPTER XII.

THE TRUTH OF CHRISTIANITY MANIFESTED BY ITS VISIBLE EFFECTS ON THE LIVES OF CHRISTIANS.

Another signal effect of the Christian religion is to be perceived in the exterior of those who profess it; for their countenance and manner constrain men to reverence them and hold them in honour. The fiercest men have become gentle, at the sight of devout Christians clad in lowly guise. Attila, the ferocious King of the Huns, beholding Saint Leo, the Pope, in the city of Ravenna, and hearing his words, abandoned the invasion of Italy. Totila, the savage King of the Goths, could not confront the poor and humble monk, St. Benedict; but, prostrating himself upon the ground, would only rise at the Saint's behest. Theodosius, the Emperor, after the slaughter of the inhabitants of Thessalonica, was by St. Ambrose banished from the temple of God, and, not daring to disobey, humbled himself and did penance. Time would fail me were I to make mention of all the examples that I can recall; but it is not necessary to enlarge upon what is so clear. Even in our own time we have seen arrogant sinners, smitten with compunction at the sight of holy men; and this compunction has led them to an entire reformation of life.

Now the cause of this effect is supernatural grace, with the infusion of all virtues. For we know how the soul can, by means of the imagination, alter the whole countenance. Thus angry feelings express themselves openly on the face : we grow pale with fear, red with shame; joy makes the eye sparkle, etc. For, as the understanding makes use of those corporeal organs, the senses; the thoughts of the understanding (when they are very intense) often stamp themselves upon the body, especially on the eyes and countenance. Thus a haughty mind can be recognized by the arrogance of a man's looks; cruelty by his rolling eye; light mindedness by restless limbs. Nay, sometimes sin can infect the very air and the bodies of others — as we see in the case of malignant old women, who can bewitch little children. Good and bad habits, when they are deeply rooted in the soul, cannot be so completely disguised that they never appear in the face. As we know that every effect expresses its cause, the beautiful and venerable aspect of perfect Christians can proceed from nothing, save from the beauty of their soul, which is, of itself, most efficacious in the conversion of sinners. Even though a man be uneducated, if he leads a holy life, he will have more influence with his fellows' than an eloquent and learned philosopher, or than miracles, either reported or witnessed. We see how attentively an audience will listen to the words of a learned preacher, without making any change in their lives; yet, although his eloquence may be much praised, it will remain barren if his life corresponds not to his words. In the same way, both in past days and in our own time, many miracles have been wrought, and crowds of men and women have flocked to see them; but they have produced but little fruit in the reformation of their lives.

A perfect Christian life on the contrary, will convert to God numberless souls, not only among the poor and simple, but among the learned, and will fill them with compunction. Indeed many have been so strongly influenced by the holiness of life exhibited by perfect Christians, that they have left the world and retired into a cloister. There must, then, be some intrinsic power in those who lead holy lives, which enables them to produce such marvelous effects. I say intrinsic, for this power is not exterior, since the body does not, strictly speaking, act upon the spirit; and therefore the exterior of a perfect Christian could not have power to change the will and the understanding of other men. The chief virtue of a perfect Christian, and that which produces both his good life and his exterior beauty, is his Faith in, and love of Christ Crucified. And the more this Faith and love increase, the more beautiful and venerable does his exterior aspect become.

Truth is stronger than falsehood. Now there is, as we have already said, no more efficacious means of inducing men to lead a good life, than the example of a good Christian. For, the example of virtuous heathens led very few to heathen perfection; whereas those who have been converted by the example of Christianity are innumerable. Hence the root and essence of the Christian religion cannot be false or futile; otherwise it would produce less effect on the lives of men than does philosophy. This, as we know, is not the case.

God is the primary Cause of motion, without which nothing moves; and, as He does all things wisely, He produces the noblest effects from the noblest causes. Therefore, as the Christian life is a most noble effect, it springs from most noble causes, of which one is the good example exhibited by this life. One begets the other, as man begets man, and animals beget animals. Therefore we must acknowledge, that the example of a good life is a most noble cause and instrument, used by God to lead men to true virtue, and that, as this virtue is Faith informed by "charity, Faith also must be true.

CHAPTER XIII.

THE TRUTH OF THE FAITH DEMONSTRATED BY THE WONDERFUL WORKS OF CHRIST, ESPECIALLY THOSE WHICH PERTAIN TO HIS POWER.

We have, by the assistance of God, proved the truth of Faith by the effects daily visible in the Church of Christ. In further confirmation of our proofs, we can bring forward further arguments, based on the works which Christ wrought in past times, and which were patent to the whole world. As philosophers investigate the natural causes of the things which they see, we will place before our eyes the Triumph of the Cross, described before. And, as philosophers, seeing the greatness and wonderful order and perfection of the Universe, believe God to be the most powerful, the wisest and most perfect Cause of causes, and Prime Mover of all things, we, likewise, from the marvels described in the Triumph of the Cross, desire to show that Christ Crucified has surpassed, in power and wisdom and goodness, all those that have been honoured and adored as gods, and has done in- comparably greater and more wonderful things than they have wrought; so that He, most surely, is "a great God, and a great King above all gods" (Ps. 94:3).

Let us then begin by considering His power, and by placing before our eyes the Triumph of the Cross. Let us argue in this wise. Either Christ is the True God and the First Cause of all things, or He is not. If He be God, it follows that Christianity is true; and there is no need for further discussion. If He be not God, He must have been the proudest man, and the greatest liar that ever lived. He must also have been exceedingly

foolish. For it would have been, indeed, the height of folly for a man, unaided by wealth or worldly power, ignorant of philosophy and of rhetoric, to attempt, merely by virtue of his death, to fight against the Divine Majesty, and to usurp to himself the honour due to It; or to strive to induce learned and powerful men to join a new religion which should change the whole face of the earth, should acknowledge him as God, and should inspire his followers with such fervent love for him, that for his sake they should be ready to lay down life itself. Could any absurdity equal such aspirations as these? If, then, Jesus of Nazareth were not true God, He would be a most foolish and sacrilegious seducer. How could such a man have been able to supersede the Law of Moses, and to struggle successfully against men of authority and learning, against the powers of heaven and hell, nay, against God Himself? Why, O Jews, did not
your God take vengeance on Him? For what reason, ye Gentiles, have your deities not overthrown Him? How has it come to pass that a poor and lowly man, put to death by Crucifixion, has accomplished such mighty deeds? What God, I speak not of men, can be compared with Christ?

Again, consider how foolish it is to draw a comparison between Jesus Christ and Apollonius, Pythagoras, Soc-rates, Caesar, or any emperor; since none of them has either proclaimed himself God, or done any deed which can be compared to the works of Christ. Mahomet, who never called himself God, attracted a barbarous people to himself by force of arms and by sensual indulgence; he spoke admiringly of Christ, but himself never proposed anything to his followers, above the force of human nature.

Jesus Christ did not act thus. His commands to men

106

are most arduous and most difficult to obey; since He would have them believe in a God, One in Nature, Three in Person. His followers must confess that the Father, the Son, and the Holy Ghost are true God, Simple Sub- stance, and that He is very God, the Son of God, One with the Father and the Holy Spirit, and True Man, the Son of the Virgin Mary, who must be reverenced as the true Mother of God. Furthermore, Christians are bound to confess that the Cross, which used to be an instrument of punishment, is a powerful sign of our salvation, and that a little bread and wine is changed, by virtue of certain words pronounced over it, into the Body and Blood of Christ, the heavenly food of our souls, and as such has to be adored. We must also believe that no one can enter into the Kingdom of God unless he receive the baptism which confers heavenly grace. And we must hold, with inviolable firmness, every point taught by Scripture, however difficult it may be to human understanding.

Neither is Faith sufficient for salvation. We must also love invisible things so much as to despise such as are visible, and to be ready to suffer persecution, and even death itself, rather than offend God in anything. Christ does not promise us in this world riches, or honour, or dignity, but rattier poverty, persecution, scourges, exile, prison, and death. He reserves for us hereafter happiness unspeakable, a share in the glory of the angels, the resurrection of the body, and joy which "eye has not seen, ear has not heard, neither has it entered into the heart of man to conceive"(1 Cor. 2:9). And although the things which our Lord sets before us are most difficult to human nature, innumerable Christians, of all times and conditions of life, have accepted His teaching, and adhered to it so closely, that they have preferred to die rather than to deny it.

Let us, then, place before our eyes Christ living in poverty, the reputed son of a carpenter; and let us question Him as to His thoughts. He will reply: I, poor though I be and an exile on earth, propose to lay down laws for the whole human race, and so to change the face of the world, that, although I shall be crucified, men shall adore Me as true God, One with the Father and the Holy Ghost. And it is My will that the cross and nails and thorny crown, and all the other instruments of My Passion, shall be honoured and held in veneration as most precious treasures. Likewise men shall believe that a little bread and wine is changed into My Body and Blood, and shall adore It as God. They shall con- fess that the water of baptism cleanses from sin, and that oil and chrism sanctify, and that My doctrine, of which it is not lawful to change one jot or tittle, surpasses all other teaching. My Virgin Mother also shall be honoured and loved throughout the whole world, and My Apostles, who were fishermen, shall be so revered, that men shall honour their very bones and ashes. If any poor man were to speak thus, should we not deride him as a mad- man?

But, if, in spite of your ridicule, He should say further : It is My will, not only that men should believe these things, but should on their account live in holiness, and should for the sake of invisible things spurn such as are visible, suffering for love of Me poverty, hunger, thirst, labour, torture and death — would you not think that He had lost His senses? And were He to add: I shall accomplish all these things against the will of the whole world, and shall overcome kings and princes, the powers of hell, and the machinations of men — would you not think Him completely mad?

But what would be your opinion of Him, if, when you asked Him with what weapons He proposed to achieve these victories, He should reply: My only arms will be the tongue, used not in rhetorical or philosophical eloquence, but in simplicity of preaching; and I know that by means of this preaching many will be converted to Me, and will for My name endure suffering and death; and the blood of My faithful will become the seed, of the Church. And so great will be the power of My doctrine that Peter the fisherman and his successors will become heads of the proud city of Rome, and the chiefs of the world; and emperors will humbly stoop to kiss their feet. And good and learned men shall, in every language, compose innumerable books filled with My praises, and in defense of My doctrine. And when my priests shall, with great reverence and solemnity, pronounce My word, all people shall listen to it, standing with bared heads. And none shall prevail against Me, but My religion shall endure forever. Would you not have treated such words as foolish. dreams? And, surely, when we consider how all these prophecies have been fulfilled, shall we not see that they could not possibly have been accomplished by one poor man, nor by all men, nor by all natural or supernatural power, but only by the infinite power of God? Beholding these things, can we possibly doubt that they are the work of God, and that the Faith of Christ is true? What conjuror, what philosopher, what powerful king has ever performed the like? Can Mahomet, can the heathen gods be compared to Christ, before whose coming none of these things were accomplished, or even imagined? Neither can we say that these marvels happened by chance, for they had been foretold years before their accomplishment by the Prophets and Sybils, whose books are known to the whole world. This is another argument in favour of the truth of Christianity.

In the course of nature some causes invariably produce their effect; others do so nearly always; and others are indifferent as to whether they produce their effect or not. Again, some arguments, i.e., those called demonstrative, infallibly constrain the understanding to accept a proposition; others almost always incline the understanding to receive it; and others sometimes appeal to the mind, and at other times produce no effect upon it. Demonstration abounds in mathematical science, though there is very little of it in natural science, and still less in moral science which treats of sublime and Divine things. For our understanding is so weak, that it does not really know the nature of things; and, therefore, it is with difficulty convinced with regard to things which are not manifest. If, then, it be difficult to persuade the understanding to embrace moral and Divine things, how much harder must it not be to incline it to virtue and contemplation, seeing how the flesh ever rebels against the spirit? But it is, above all things, difficult to incline the intellect to per- severance in good works. In philosophical schools we see many systems under many founders; but few sincerely love what they learn or teach. For, very few who know what really are good works, are, as a consequence, by their knowledge of them, attracted to persevere in their performance. If, then, the greatest philosophers, with all their learning and eloquence, have scarcely succeeded in persuading a few men to believe things dictated by reason
— such as, for instance, God's providence over human affairs and the duty of practicing virtue and avoiding vice — how much less able would they have been to induce men to believe things above natural reason, and above all, to love good works? But the disciples of Christ, unknown fishermen, were able, by their simple preaching, to persuade the world to accept the truths of faith and to

110

love these truths so ardently, and to pursue good works so unflaggingly, that in comparison with them they esteemed all earthly things as dust and ashes, and refused to deny their faith either for promises or threats, or even for death itself. Surely, if Christianity were false, the Apostles could not more easily have persuaded men to accept it, than philosophers had induced them to embrace systems which appealed to natural reason. And the words of the poor fishermen would not alone have sufficed to convert the world, but those words must needs have been con- firmed by miracles. And who but God could have enabled them to work their miracles, which surpassed all the powers of human nature? But, supposing that the Apostles worked no miracles at all, surely the wonder of wonders? Would be that a crucified man should be able, by means of twelve poor fishermen, to persuade, by words alone, the entire world to embrace His doctrine. Therefore, whether the spread of Christianity be due to miracles or not, we cannot deny that the power of Christ has been beyond any natural power. And, since the First Cause is

that which is more powerful than other causes, so the true God must be He that is more mighty than any other god. Therefore, Jesus Christ, whose Faith has been victorious over all other forms of religion, must be the true God, and His teaching must be the true religion.

CHAPTER XIV.

THE TRUTH OF CHRISTIANITY SHOWN BY ARGUMENTS BASED ON THE WISDOM OF CHRIST

The property of wisdom is a capacity to subordinate things to their end. Thus, that artist is considered a master who can dispose the circumstances of his art towards the end which he wishes to attain; and it is to the architect, and not to the builders, that the credit of an edifice is due. But artists, seeing that they only work towards some particular end, are relatively, not absolutely, wise. He alone who labours for the last end of human life, and who directs all his activities towards the attainment of that end, is endowed with absolute wisdom. Now, as Jesus of Nazareth has pointed out the true end of human life, and the true means of attaining thereto, and has done so with a clearness and a force exercised by no other man, He alone can be called truly and pre-eminently wise.

Again. As power to beget children is a sign of perfect virility, so power to teach is a mark of perfect wisdom. And, surely, never has teacher arisen whose doctrine is more sublime, or more useful, than is that of Christ; and never has one taught with ease and power comparable to His. The systems of philosophers are obscure, and mingled with many errors; and the teachers themselves are uncertain on many points, such as Divine Providence,the end of human life, and the things which pertain to salvation. But our Saviour, Jesus. Christ, has enlightened even women and children, to understand clearly many things incomprehensible to philosophers, and has enabled them to hold His doctrine with a firmness invincible even by death.

Further. As the power of an agent is known by the extent and duration of his work, the wisdom of a teacher is recognized by the number of ignorant sinners whom he converts, and the speed wherewith their conversion is effected. For it is no great sign of power to attract those who are naturally and habitually well disposed; but only great wisdom can instruct, in a short time, men of mean understanding, and women and children, and can reform notorious sinners. Christ alone has succeeded in effecting these wonders throughout the whole world. Therefore, He alone is endowed with incomparable wisdom.

Again. It is no great thing to produce natural effects by natural causes. For example, it does not surprise us if a conflagration be caused by fire, but it would be marvelous were it produced by water. Hence, it is only supreme and infinite power that can act on natural objects, either without instruments or with such as are diametrically opposed to the effect produced; or that can operate on all natural objects with the same instrument. Thus it is nothing very wonderful that philosophers should have been able to teach by means of ordinary methods; but only Supreme Power could have taught by means of that which, in the world, is accounted foolishness. Now Christ, by means of the folly and
the ignominy of the Cross, has imparted to men sublime wisdom, true wisdom, which can only be acquired by the teaching of the Cross, wisdom, compared to which all human learning is foolishness. Therefore, the wisdom of Christ must itself be pre-eminent.

If wisdom, mean the science of Divine things, the wisdom of Christ must exceed all other wisdom. For, as we see by comparing Christian doctrine with philosophical systems, no one has treated of Divine things so fully, or so sublimely, as Christ has done. Theology has purged philosophy, and made it perfect, and has diffused so widely the knowledge of the Divine, that Christians, even the least educated, easily understand points which are stumbling-blocks to philosophers. And, further, the preaching of the Apostles has illuminated the world to see its errors. Since this dawn of the light of Christ, philosophers and poets, ashamed of their false gods and fables, have tried to disguise their superstitions under a cloak of allegory.

Again. It is only great wisdom that can understand sublime and intricate matters. Christ has taught and easily defended, most subtle doctrine. How, then, shall we hesitate to declare His wisdom incomparable? His doctrine has not only stood the test of argument, but likewise that of cruel persecution, under which philoso-phers would "have denied their first principles. For as their philosophy proceeded from natural reason, they would have had neither strength nor wisdom to uphold it.

But the teaching of Christ, being supernatural, is likewise, of necessity, invincible. Christianity is either false or true. If it be true, discussion is at an end. If it be false, Christ must still be acknowledged to have been the wisest of men, seeing that He was able to persuade men to accept doctrines, difficult and unpalatable, and to adhere to them so firmly, that no human reason or power' has been able to uproot them from the world. Nevertheless, in all that Christ has taught there is nothing repugnant to philosophy or to science. On the contrary, Christianity culls truth from all systems, even from paganism. If Christ had not been Wisdom Itself, He could never have founded so wise a religion as is this. If His doctrine had been false, it would not be defensible by science. For philosophers find it sufficiently difficult to defend even truth against their opponents. Even were we obliged to acknowledge Christianity to be a falsehood, we should still be constrained to recognize the extraordinary sagacity of its Founder, who by means of subtle fallacies has been able to lead His disciples to sublime perfection of life. But, seeing that there can be no harmony between virtue and deceit, and no agreement between truth and falsehood, we are driven to confess that Christ is truly wise, with a wisdom surpassing that of men. His wisdom is attested by the many who have extolled it, not only by their words and writing, but by their works, and by the shedding of their blood.

Finally. The greatest power of wise men appears, chiefly, in the fact, that they require but a short time in which to lead their pupils to the perfection of knowledge.

But as no one has given such clear proofs of this power as Christ has manifested, it is evident that He alone is wise above all men. Every science is either rational or real. By rational science we understand logic, rhetoric and poetry; and the end aimed at by these branches of rational science is to teach us to weave together arguments, chains of reasoning, and exhortations, which will convert men to agree with our opinions. Now, Christ instructed the Apostles in rational science to such good purpose, that, by their preaching, they exercised more influence in the world, than had ever been achieved by any human power or learning. Real science is either practical and moral or speculative, Christ has taught practical and moral science so effectually, that Christians need no philosophy but His. Speculative science may be concerned with Divine things, and in the teaching of Christ is contained such fullness of Divine knowledge that, beside it, all human wisdom is stultified. Or, on the other hand, it may teach the knowledge of numbers and of figures, as do arithmetic and geometry; but as this knowledge is in no wise necessary to salvation, the teaching of Christ disregards it, except for purposes of allegory. Thirdly, speculative science may treat of sensible things, in order, by means of them, to lead men to speculation on intelligible things. The teaching of Christ exhibits most perfectly this speculative science, seeing that His preaching abounds in the use of visible things, as images or mirrors of such as are invisible. Thus we see that Christ only is supremely wise, since He only has been able, easily, to lead men to the fullness of knowledge.

Again. The pleasures of the mind are far greater than those of the senses; but the greatest of all intellectual enjoyments is the contemplation of Supreme Truth. Therefore, since wisdom consists in the cognition and contemplation of this Truth, he must be wisest who most delights in it, Now, never has the contemplation of Truth been so ardently loved, and so strenuously sought after, as in these days, when, for its sake, men abandon every earthly joy, and, living like disembodied spirits, heed not the things of the flesh, and are disturbed at no tribulation. Thus do they prove that Christ, their Teacher, is wise beyond all human wisdom, and beyond all the wisdom of heathen deities, yea, that He is the very Wisdom of the Eternal God.

CHAPTER XV.

THE TRUTH OF CHRIST'S TEACHING IS PROVED BY HIS GOODNESS.

We have shown that Jesus of Nazareth surpasses, in wisdom and in power, all men and all heathen deities. Hence, if we believe in the existence of any god. He only can be that God. It will next be our duty to prove His Divinity by arguments founded on His goodness, and to show that Jesus Christ is the Supreme Good and the End of human life. And we must premise that all human operations, i.e., such as proceed from free will, are effected for some end; for appetite always tends to that which either is good, or appears to be good. It cannot tend to two things as to its ultimate end; for it is so fully satisfied by its last end, that it can desire nothing which is not ordered thereto. Now, as men, though not all of the same opinion or endowed with the same degree of knowledge, are yet all of the same nature, they must all tend to the same end, which is happiness; although, from their difference of condition, they do not all place their happiness in the same thing. If, then, we can prove that Christ is the Last End, to which all nature tends, it will be clear that He must be the very Truth, the First Cause, the Supreme Good, and in fact the true God.

In order to make this argument more clear, we must remember, that, when one thing tends naturally to another as to its end, it will be hindered in the attainment of this end, if it be joined by another thing of a contrary nature.

Thus, if a heavy thing move towards its centre, it will be impeded in its course if it be joined to a light thing whose tendency it is to go upwards. Thus birds, whose bodies are heavy are nevertheless raised aloft by their wings; whereas, a merely heavy thing moves swiftly towards its centre. Now, as man is composed of a corporeal and a spiritual nature, it happens, that, while his spiritual nature tends to true beatitude, his senses, disturb and trouble him in the pursuit of his end; and, although they cannot force him to evil, they often incline him to inordinate desires. From these molestations, and from the weakness of his understanding, arise the divers human conceptions of happiness. If we would learn, by means of man's natural desire, in what his beatitude consists, we must not consider the desires and inclinations of such as live like beasts, but of such as live according to reason. Just as, if we want to see whether heavy things move downwards or upwards, we must not choose birds as a test; but must select something completely heavy. We may learn what is the Last End of man by examining the desires of such as have purified themselves from the defilement of the senses, and who live according to reason. And as no life is so pure and so reasonable as the Christian life, we can, from the desires common to Christians, learn what is the Last End of man. Now, as Christians^ unite in an intense love for Christ Crucified, as the Last End of human life, it follows that we cannot reasonably hold that any but Christ can be the Last End of man."

Again. Man's last end is his ultimate perfection; and the more perfect he becomes, the nearer does he approach to his end. Now, nothing causes man to become so perfect in life and in contemplation, as does Jesus Christ Crucified; and they who least resemble Him and are the most remote from Him, are the worst and most imperfect of men. He, therefore, must be the Last End of human life.

Further. The desire of the last end is natural to everything, and is ineradicable. When, therefore, men, who are purged from vice desire something, they love it so much that all other things appear to them as naught in comparison with the object of their desire. They would rather die than relinquish their pursuit of it. Now, as the life of true Christians is a pure life, and as they desire Christ Crucified with so steadfast a desire that they would sacrifice life itself rather than lose His love, and would most gladly die for His sake, it is manifest that Christ is the Supreme Truth and the Last End of human life. Our argument is further strengthened by the fact, that nothing is so steadfastly desired as He. For when men love other things, they love them not more than themselves, but for their own satisfaction; and would rather abandon them than die for their sake.

We see, likewise, how all things of the same species incline naturally to the same end; as all heavy things tend towards their centre. Therefore, Christ must be the Last End of human life, since nothing has been pursued by men with the same ardor and constancy, that they have shown in following Him. This is the reason why Christians are so closely united together; for we "see that they love Jesus Christ above all things. For His sake they likewise love each other, of whatso-ever race and country they may be; and the more their faith in Christ increases, the stronger grows their brotherly love. This could not be the case were their faith not true. For fallacy and error cause, not harmony, but discord.

Again. The soul enjoys greater happiness in pro-portion as, by love and contemplation, it draws nearer to its last end. But the happiness enjoyed by Christians far surpasses all pleasures of understanding and sense. This truth is proved by the invincible constancy of the martyrs, who went to death rejoicing and exulting; by the numberless monks and hermits who, relinquishing all things, and living in the practice of the greatest austerity, have yet enjoyed incomparable happiness; and by the numerous philosophers who have found such delight in the study of Holy Scripture, that, in order to devote themselves to it, they have abandoned every other branch of learning. Hence we see that the joy which souls find in Christ exceeds all other happiness.

If, then, felicity be synonymous with proximity-to-our last end, Christ, in whom all happiness is found, must be the Last End of human life.

In order to comprehend, collectively, all the properties of our Last End we reason thus. As all things of the same species tend naturally to the same end, be it proximate or ultimate, it follows that men, who are all of the same species, must be fitted for some one thing which is the common end of human life. Now, all men agree in professing that they tend towards a last end; but they differ as to that wherein their last end is to be found. But since the happiness of mankind consists in the act of understanding, it is natural to conclude that this last end is to be found in that thing, towards which they who live the most rationally and whose affections are the most purified do uniformly incline; that to which they steadfastly adhere, loving it better than themselves; delighting in it; drawing from it sanctity of ways and brightness of heavenly life; and being raised by its influence so far above this world, that, in comparison with their end, they repute all earthly things as worthless. Now, as all these wonderful effects have never been produced in man by any, save by Christ Crucified, He must be the Last End of human life.

But why do we insist on so self-evident a truth knowing, as we do, that it is the property of Good to communicate itself, and that the graces and blessings diffused by Christ over mankind are absolutely unequalled? His coming has purged the world from error, filled it with sanctity and virtue, and communicated to all His followers happiness which no earthly thing could give. His supreme goodness is further shown by the promptitude and liberality wherewith He not only forgives sinners, but so enriches them with His gifts, that where sin did
abound, grace has much more abounded, and they who return to Him from their sins are enabled to lead a virtuous life and enjoy their pristine peace and happiness, whereas they who forsake Him lose all tranquility of mind. What further proof do we require that Christ is the Supreme Good, and the Last End of man?

CHAPTER XVI.

THE TRUTH OF CHRISTIANITY IS PROVED BY THE POWER, WISDOM, AND GOODNESS OF CHRIST, CONSIDERED COLLECTIVELY.

We may sum up in a few words what has been already said about the power, the wisdom, and the goodness of Christ. Had Christ not been God, He would have been the most proud and the most foolish of men. And if (as some hold) the assertion of His Divinity was not made by Himself but by His disciples how can a religion of such goodness, wisdom, and power, be the outcome of such a falsehood? If Christ be not God, who is God? God preserves and governs all inferior things by the requisite means; and, as no means are so suitable for the attainment of a virtuous life as the Faith and love of our Saviour Jesus Christ, we must either acknowledge that He is the true means whereby we attain beatitude, or must hold, with fatalists, that things happen by chance; and we must end in denying the existence of God.

Again. If there be any true religion in the world; and if no religion be supported by such arguments and undeniable proofs as is the Christian religion; where, save in Christianity, are we to seek the true religion?

Further. No religion has endured the constant and cruel persecution inflicted on Christianity^ Other religions, or rather superstitions, have never roused in the world the hatred excited by the Faith of Christ. Yet, in spite of this fact, other religions which persecuted Christianity, have died out, of themselves, without being persecuted. Christianity has only flourished, and waxed stronger, by means of its conflicts. How do we account for this fact, if Christianity be untrue?

We must remember, likewise, that they who have persecuted Christians have been, not good and upright men, but men of infamous life. Is not this a further proof of the truth of our religion?

Again. No religion has made converts under the same conditions as those in which men have accepted the Faith of Christ. For those who have become Christians have done so, not in hopes of gaining riches, or honour, or pleasure, but with the expectation of having to bear poverty and shame, torture and death. If these men had not been enlightened by true light, could they have acted thus?

This collection of arguments, surely, ought to convince all men of the truth of Christianity. For, although the intellect may not be persuaded by one proof, nor by two, nor by three, a series of proofs carries as much weight as does a chain of mathematical demonstrations, or the sight of a dead man raised to life.

If, then, Christianity be true, all other religions must be false; for none can be saved except by Faith. This condition for salvation is a most reasonable one; for our beatitude is to consist in the vision and fruition of God, to which none can attain, save by the supernatural gift of Faith, without which, as St. Paul says, "it is impossible to please God"(Heb. 11:6). Neither have they any ground for excuse or complaint who live in distant lands, where Christianity is unknown. For, as all men are endowed with reason, which leads to the knowledge of God, and as God further manifests Himself in the natural order of Creation, it follows that if any one live according to reason, and turn to God for help (as nature teaches every effect to turn to its cause), Almighty God, the Supreme Good who is never wanting to any necessity of, even His irrational, creatures, will still less fail man in matters pertaining to salvation. He will rather enlighten him, either by interior inspiration, as He enlightened Job; or by the ministry of angels, as He instructed Cornelius the Centurion; or by preaching, as He taught the Eunuch of Candace, by means of Philip the Apostle.

BOOK III.

METHOD OBSERVED THROUGHOUT THIS BOOK.

We have already proved the truth of Christianity by means of arguments based on the past and present works of Christ. But it is our duty, not merely to demonstrate the solid foundations of our Faith, but, also, to defend it against the objections raised against it; and to show that, while it teaches many things surpassing human understanding, not one point of its doctrine is either unreasonable or, incredible.

We will, then, first, discuss the articles of our belief. Next, we will examine the reasons for the divers moral commandments imposed upon us. Thirdly, we will demonstrate the equity of the laws, of which Christianity makes use in judging. And lastly, we will explain the hidden meaning of the ceremonies used in our religious rites.

It is true that many learned writers have treated these points, fully and eloquently, but we could not omit them in our work, without leaving it imperfect. And, whereas other authors have handled these matters with great diffuseness and subtlety; it is our intention to set them forth so simply, and so briefly, as to make them easily intelligible, not only to the learned, but to the ignorant and unbelieving.

CHAPTER I.

GOD CONTAINS WITHIN HIMSELF, AND CAN PERFORM, AN INFINITE NUMBER OF THINGS SURPASSING HUMAN UNDERSTANDING.

If we think, for a moment, of the natural weakness of our intellect, we shall easily see that in God there must be many things which exceed our mental capacity. We believe that the acme of human wisdom has been reached by a certain number of great philosophers; yet even they acknowledge themselves to be baffled by some purely natural phenomena. If, then, men of the very highest order of intelligence have been able to attain merely to a very imperfect knowledge of the everyday things of nature, how can we expect to understand heavenly mysteries, and the Divine truths which are so far above any earthly intelligence?

Again. Although men are all of the same species, they differ so much in mental capacity, that many, although making every effort, could never succeed in understanding matters which are comparatively simple to others. Why then should we wonder, if the angelic mind be so differentiated from the human, that angels know many things which men are quite incapable of comprehending? And as God is infinitely superior to angels, must there not be in Him infinite things surpassing the powers of human reason? And although we can, as a rule, know a cause by its effects; yet when a cause greatly exceeds its effects, the effects do but most imperfectly manifest their cause. Hence, God, being infinitely superior to His effects, can only be ~most imperfectly known by them.

It is not difficult, furthermore, to prove that God can do infinite things of which the human intellect is incapable. For, as all our knowledge begins from the senses, our intellect can only, naturally, grasp such things as are made clear to it by means of the senses; and whatever efforts we may make, we can never know anything which exceeds the natural order, or which is beyond our imagination. Now, God, being Pure Act and Infinite Power, is not tied down to any order whatsoever, but infinitely exceeds all created things, both spiritual and corporeal. Thus we are constrained to acknowledge, that He can do infinite things which we can never understand} We know, further, not only that He can do, but that He has done many such things, viz., things spiritual and angelic.

We can assign three reasons which make it fitting that God should have done, and should have manifested to the "world many supernatural things, surpassing the capacity of human understanding. First He has done so with a view to the salvation of mankind. For, as man is made for God, and for a supernatural end, he could not attain to that end, were it not revealed to him by God, together with the means conducive to it. Secondly. God has acted thus, in order to humble man and to teach him to know his own nothingness as compared to the Divine Majesty. For, in proportion as we realize that we can neither know nor contemplate (save most imperfectly) even things revealed to us, we shall become more lowly minded, and more reverent towards such as are Divine.

Thirdly. By the manifold revelation of His mysteries, which God has made to the world, man has acquired a great relish for eternal truths, and has learned to love the Divine goodness and condescension.

Hence, the fact that we cannot understand the truths of Christianity is no reason for rejecting these truths. It is a reason, rather, for making a serious study of the religion which teaches them, and of thus proving to ourselves that it contains nothing either unreasonable or incredible, But to make this more evident, we will (in the succeeding chapters) descend to particular instances.

CHAPTER II.

AN EXAMINATION OF CERTAIN ARTICLES OF THE CHRISTIAN CREED WHICH EXCEED THE LIMITS OF HUMAN UNDERSTANDING.

We may divide the articles of belief peculiar to Christians, into those that pertain to the Divinity of Christ, and those that concern His Humanity.

Regarding His Divinity, we believe that there are not many gods, but one only God. This, the fundamental doctrine of Christianity, is not merely believed, but also known, by enlightened and learned men. Secondly. Together with the Unity, we believe in the Trinity of God, by which we mean, that the Father, the Son, and the Holy Ghost, are One God and Three Persons. These two articles regard the Divine Essence. The next articles refer to the Divine works. And, first, considering the works of nature, we profess that God has created all things, or made them out of nothing. Next, passing to the works which He has wrought in the supernatural order, we declare, that God alone can sanctify the creature, and that He does so, by means of supernatural gifts, in order to draw the creature to Himself We next pass to the works of glory. Considering the glory of the soul, we profess that such as have been sanctified by God, will, after death, be glorified in beatitude and supernatural fruition, and that the body will rise again. We also acknowledge the immortality and glorification of the bodies of the just, and the damnation of the wicked.

Concerning the Humanity of Christ, we believe that Christ is true God and true Man — Son of God, and Son of the Virgin Mary, by her conceived and borne, through the power of the Holy Ghost; that for our salvation He was crucified, died, and was buried. We believe, moreover, that He went down to that part of hell called Limbo, thence to deliver the souls of the Patriarchs; that He rose again from death to glory, and ascended into

Heaven, where He sits at the right hand of the Father; and that He will come again to judge the living and the dead, and to make new the whole face of the earth.

Thus, our whole faith consists in these twelve articles. We also believe all that is embraced in the Holy Scriptures, and all that the holy Roman Church has defined, or shall hereafter define. We shall, therefore, proceed to discuss these twelve articles of the Creed, and to show that they contain nothing, either unreasonable, or incredible. We have not made any mention of the Blessed Sacrament of the Altar nor of the other Sacraments; but they are included under the head of the sanctification of the rational creature, and we shall further treat of them when we are explaining the ceremonies of the Church. We have already spoken of the Unity of God, in the First Article of the First Book. Therefore, we shall not treat of it now, more especially as the greatest of the philosophers, and indeed nearly all men, agree with us in admitting this truth.

CHAPTER III.

THE MYSTERY OF THE TRINITY IS NEITHER UN-REASONABLE NOR INCREDIBLE.

PASSING over the first principle of the Christian Faith, viz., the unity of God, we will proceed to the second article which is pre-eminently difficult, viz., the Unity in Trinity. By this we mean that the three Persons, — Father, Son, and Holy Ghost, — are not three Gods or three natures, but One God and One Nature."We hold that There is One God, of most pure nature; and our belief is in no wise contrary to philosophy. Although we believe that the Father, the Son and the Holy Ghost are One God, we do not teach, as Sabellius taught, that one Person is called at one time Father, at one time Son, and at another time Holy Ghost. Nor, do we hold, as was held by Arius, that the three Persons, are substantially different, and that the Son is inferior and posterior to the Father, and the Holy Ghost inferior and posterior to the Father and the Son. We profess, against Sabellius, that the Father, the Son, and the Holy Ghost are three distinct Persons. We teach, against Arius, that they are of one and the same nature, and equal in power and glory; so that all that belongs to the Father, belongs likewise to the Son and to the Holy Ghost; and all that belongs to the Son, belongs equally to the Father and the Holy Ghost; and all that belongs to the Holy Ghost, belongs, in like manner, to the Father and the Son. Thus, there is not between the Divine Persons the natural distinction which exists among creatures, consequent upon the more or less that each possesses, but merely a relative distinction. By which we mean that the Father possesses all that He has, of Himself, and from none other; that the Son, who has all that the Father has, derives it from the Father; and that the Holy Ghost, who has all that have the Father and the Son, receives it from Father and Son. Nor, on this account, are the Son and the Holy Ghost inferior to the Father, for they are One with Him in Nature and in dignity. Neither did the Father exist before the Son, nor the Son before the Holy Ghost. For, God, being immutable and eternal, the Father could not be God before He was the Father, and was always God and Father; and as He could not be Father without a Son, the Son is necessarily co-eternal with Him; and as the Holy Ghost is love, and the Father and the Son have loved each other from all eternity, they can never have existed without breathing forth the Holy Ghost. Neither is there any composition in the Divine Essence; for we believe that each of the Persons is One and the Same with the Divine Nature. Human reason cannot understand how in God, who is Pure Act and Simple Substance, there can be three Persons so completely distinct that One is not the Other, so that the Father is not the Son, nor the Son the Father, nor the Holy Ghost the Father and the Son, nor the Father and the Son the Holy

Ghost; and yet at the same time the Father is the same Simple Nature as the Son, and the Son as the Father, and the Holy Ghost as the Father and the Son. For in God there is Personal, but not natural, distinction; and as we name things according to our knowledge of them, and knowing God by means of creatures, we name Him by names derived from creatures. Now, among creatures, the production of one living being from another living being is called generation, and the one who begets is termed father, and the one begotten, son. And as in God, one living Person proceeds from another living Person, we term this procession generation, and He from whom the other Person proceeds is called

THE Father, and the Person who proceeds we name THE Son. This generation, unlike that of men and animals, is wholly spiritual and Divine. And therefore we say that the Son is THE Word, the Image, and THE Begotten Wisdom of the Father. But the procession of the Holy Ghost, who is Love, is from the Father and the Son, because love is the union between the lover and the beloved, and thus the Holy Ghost proceeds immediately from two perfect Persons, the Father and the Son. But because, in the order of nature, nothing can be found which proceeds immediately from two equally perfect beings, no special name has been found for the Holy Ghost and His procession; and therefore the general term procession has been retained. It is correct, however, to call this procession the spiration of the Father and the Son, because the Holy Ghost proceeds by love, which implies a certain impetus, or breathing forth, towards the thing beloved. It is for this reason that the Person proceeding from the Father and the Son is called, par excellence, THE HOLY Spirit, although both the Father and the Son are equally Spirits and equally Holy. And because in intellectual nature, there are but two processions — the one by means of the understanding, the other by means of the will — faith reasonably teaches that in God there are but two processions and three Persons.

Anyone who desires to learn more about the mystery of the Holy Trinity, will find inexhaustible treasures of knowledge in the writings of the Fathers. We have stated only the mere substance of the Faith, and have been content to show that in the mystery of the Blessed Trinity there is nothing incredible or unreasonable. Faith teaches nothing contrary to reason, but merely declares, that we cannot, by natural reason alone, arrive at the knowledge of Divine things. For human reason can only, by means of creatures, know God as the Cause and Principle of created things. And, as God is the Principle and Cause of things, only by means of His Power, Wisdom, and Goodness, and as the three Divine Persons are not distinct in these attributes, but united in them, it follows that reason cannot, by means of creatures, apprehend the distinction of the Persons of the Blessed Trinity. We do not say that we should not believe this mystery because we cannot understand It.

For it is most foolish to gauge truth by our intellectual capacity; since in God there are infinite mysteries, unfathomable by the mind of man.

If we further consider the arguments set forth in the second Book, we can have no doubt as to the Mystery of the Trinity. Our faith in it is confirmed by certain peculiar reasons, one being that though this Mystery is above our reason, it is, in no sense, contrary to it, and that it is further rendered credible by the likeness borne to it by many created things. First, by means of the procession or emanation of creatures, the mind may rise in some sort to the contemplation of the Divine Procession.

For, in creatures we see processions of many kinds, of which those that belong to the more perfect nature are likewise most perfect and most interior. For example, there is in inanimate things a certain sort of generation. One fire generates another, the virtue of the generating fire passing into the one generated. This procession, however, is not perfect nor intrinsic; for it does not remain in the thing that generates, but passes into an object outside of itself Plants, being

animated, have procession more perfect and more intrinsic; for that which is generated from a plant belongs
to the principle of the plant producing it, and is united
to it. But here, as the thing produced is finally separated
from the principle of the producer, this procession is not
perfect nor intrinsic. As animals are more perfect than
plants, we find in them more perfect and more intrinsic
procession, and one rather spiritual than corporeal.
Now, this procession is the operation of the senses which
remains within the senses themselves. Nevertheless this
operation, being caused by an extrinsic object, its procession is not wholly intrinsic. But the procession of the
intellect is far more perfect and more interior; because,
since the intellect of itself, and by no external aid, understands that which it understands, it forms its own
operations within itself, produces the word and the likeness of the thing known, and is united, as it were, by love
to that thing in such a way as to become an image of the
Trinity — to wit : by understanding, word, and love.

But, since all our knowledge has its origin in sense, the
processions of our intellect are not wholly, but only
partly, extrinsic. We shall find, if we consider the angelic
in- tellect, that in it the procession of word and of love
is more intrinsic and more perfect than is the case in the
human intellect; because angelic cognition does not arise
from sense, but is wholly interior. Nevertheless, as the
whole of the angelic substance depends on God, we cannot
say that the procession of word and of under- standing
in the angelic intellect is as intrinsic as if it depended
on nothing extrinsic; and, therefore, it contains some
imperfection. Knowing then, as we do, that creatures
are noble in proportion as they are perfect and intrinsic,
and understanding, likewise, that every effect endeavors
to imitate its cause, our Faith surely teaches nothing

unreasonable when it professes that, as the nobility of God infinitely surpasses the nobility of all creatures, there are in Him most perfect and intrinsic
processions, arising from no extrinsic cause, and having no existence apart from His Substance; and that all creatures endeavour, in so far as they can, to imitate these processions, though they can never equal them in perfection, since the Divine Persons depend on nothing, but are God, the Cause of all things. We see, therefore, that the dogma of the Blessed Trinity contains nothing either impossible, or unreasonable.

There exists in the spiritual part of man's nature a certain likeness to the Trinity, viz., understanding, word, and love. This likeness becomes more apparent when man is engaged in actual contemplation of God; for, then, his understanding is informed by the Divine light and presence representing the Father; he forms in his contemplation a concept of God which represents the Son and is called the word of the mind; and the Divine love which springs from his understanding and his concept of God represents the Holy Spirit. Of course this human trinity is very remote from the Trinity of God, and differs from it exceedingly. For our intellectual word, and our love, are changeable, and are not the
substance of our soul; whereas the Divine Word and the Divine Love are eternal, consubstantial with the Father. But in spite of this essential difference, so vivid a likeness to the Blessed Trinity is apparent in the nobler creatures that it is proved, that this doctrine is completely in accord with reason.

This likeness to the Blessed Trinity exists, not only in the superior, but also in the inferior, ranks of creation, since the perfection of every creature consists in three things, viz., beginning, middle, and end. The beginning is attributed to the Father, the middle to the Son, and the end to the Holy Ghost. We see, likewise, in creatures another trinity, that, namely, of substance, power, and operation. We might point out many other illustrations of the trace left by the Trinity upon creatures, and of their tendency to reproduce the number three, as if it were the sum of their perfection. Aristotle, the Prince of Peripatetics, following not faith but reason, says in his Heaven and Earth: "All things appear to be made up of threes". And Pythagoras also concludes, that "all things are determined and perfected in this number three, which represents beginning, middle, and end, "and that "this number has been transferred from creatures to the gods". And "if we speak of two things (he adds) we do not mean the sum total of things; but when we say three things we mean all things; for without the third thing, the quantity would be incomplete, and therefore imperfect, since perfection means completeness". Pythagoras further adds, that "bodies being composed of three things — to wit length, breadth, and height — are perfect quantities". By these examples, and by the arguments already brought forward, it becomes clear, that our belief in the Blessed Trinity is not unreasonable, but rather that this doctrine is a most credible, and, even according to our human standard, a most probable one. For, although far exceeding human reason, it is in no wise opposed to natural philosophy. It avails itself of the arguments of philosophy, thereby giving a most sure sign of its truth.

CHAPTER IV.

THE CHRISTIAN DOCTRINE OF CREATION NEITHER INCREDIBLE NOR UNREASONABLE.

We have hitherto considered the supernatural in its relation to God. We will now look at it as it regards creatures. And first, as everyone acknowledges that God is the Efficient Cause, on whom both heaven and earth depend, it is neither untrue nor irrational to say, that God has created all things in time, or that a certain principle has out of nothing made all things, both visible and invisible. For what is an efficient cause, save a cause that gives being to its effects? And is not the most perfect cause, that which acts upon the most numerous and the most remote things? God, therefore, being Pure and Perfect, exercises His power over the being of all things. Consequently, all things depend on Him.

It is true that, in earthly things, imperfection precedes perfection. Nevertheless, speaking strictly, perfection always precedes imperfection; because every imperfect thing depends upon the perfect. God, therefore, being the most pure and perfect Act, precedes all things, and all things are made by Him.

We believe, further, and most reasonably, that all things were made out of nothing, without any pre-existing matter. For, although all things in nature and in art require material on which to operate, God, being the universal cause of all effects, gives being to all things, and as being is a universal effect, it can be pro-duced only by the universal Cause, who is God. Nothing can exist that has not been produced by Him; and even those things which are made out of matter, owe their being to Him who gave being to that matter. For all matter is either made out of something, or out of nothing.

If it be made out of nothing, our proposition is proved. If it be made out of something, that something must likewise have been made out of something else. So that we must finally accept either the hypothesis of creation out of nothing, or that of eternal matter. This latter alternative is so unreasonable, that we are driven to the former, namely, that all things were created originally out of nothing; and, that from created matter other creatures have been produced. And as God acts, not from necessity but by free will, it is not necessary to say, that the world was created from eternity; but that it was made at the time chosen by the Divine Wisdom. The reason for creation in time, is hidden in the inscrutable counsels of the Most High. We can, however, in some measure, see its congruity with the Divine Nature and its utility to man. God has done all things for the good of His elect. Now this good consists, above all, in the knowledge of God; and man can know God more perfectly through His having created the world in time, than if He had created it from all eternity. For, the fact that the world was created in time, shows that. God is infinitely perfect and infinitely happy in Himself, and that He "has no need of creatures; otherwise He would not have deferred their creation. Thus, the Christian Faith teaches nothing incredible, nor irrational, about creation.

We will now dismiss this subject. It has been amply treated by the doctors of the Church, who have pulverized the frivolous arguments whereby Aristotle, and other philosophers, have sought to prove the eternity of this world.

CHAPTER V.

THE CHRISTIAN TEACHING CONCERNING THE SANCTIFICATION, GLORY, AND RESURRECTION OF RATIONAL CREATURES CONTAINS NO ARTICLE WHICH IS EITHER IMPOSSIBLE, OR UNREASONABLE.

We have already spoken of the sanctification of man by grace, pointing out that, as man is destined for a super-natural end, to which he cannot attain save by Divine grace, this grace is supplied to Him by God, who is never found wanting to His creatures. We have likewise treated, at sufficient length, of the glory of the soul, when we proved that the end of human life is the vision of the Divine essence in the light of glory. Thus have we shown that the teaching of Faith concerning the sanctification and glory of the rational creature, is both reasonable and credible. The same may also be affirmed of the doctrine of the resurrection of the dead. For, although this could not naturally take place, since nature can only give life by generation, the Divine Power being infinite, and not limited to natural operation, can perform innumerable other things in infinite ways. Therefore, to God the resurrection of the body is most easy. Why should not He who has made all things out of nothing, be able, by raising the dead, to make one thing out of another thing? Deaths does not mean annihilation. The soul remains immortal; and the matter of which the body is formed is changed into other matter. .Even were it resolved into nothing, God could call that nothingness back to life, as easily as He could create the world out of nothing.

Hence, we shall see, on reflection, that belief in the resurrection of the body is neither absurd nor impossible, but on the contrary reasonable, expedient, and necessary. Because, as the soul is the form of the body and is immortal, its separation from the body is unnatural. Now, as any unnatural condition is incongruous with the Divine Wisdom, it cannot be permanent; and therefore the soul must of necessity return to the body.

Again. Without the body, the being of the soul is imperfect, All things tend to their perfection. Therefore, without the resurrection of the body, the soul could never be completely happy, since its desire for perfection (which consists in the union of soul with body), would remain eternally unsatisfied.

Further. Happiness is due to those that live aright; and, in this life, it is not the soul which lives but the man. Life, intelligence, and all other activities are not attributes of the soul alone, but of the whole man. It is the whole man who acts, and the soul is the form, by virtue whereof he acts. Happiness, therefore, is due not only to the soul, but to the whole man who lives aright. Now, without the resurrection of the body, the soul only would receive reward.

"Furthermore. Since Divine Providence rewards the good and punishes the guilty; and since the body, as well as the soul, does good and evil, the body equally deserves punishment or reward. But if the body rise not again, how is justice to be satisfied?

The foregoing arguments, besides proving the reasonableness of our faith in the resurrection of the body, demonstrate further that the body must rise to immortality. — Otherwise, each death would necessitate a corresponding resurrection, and the series would continue ad infinitum.

We believe, likewise, that the body will rise to glory. For matter must be proportionate to its form, and if the soul, which is the form of the body, be glorified, the body must receive proportionate glory. For it would not be fitting that the glorified soul should be joined to a body not glorified, nor subject in obedience. Therefore, Faith most logically teaches that, by the power of God, the glory of the soul overflows into the Body, rendering it agile, completely obedient to the soul, and absolutely perfect.

And, since all bodies are made for man, who is their end, faith teaches, likewise, that when man is glorified, the whole world will also be glorified, since things must needs become proportioned to the end for which they are destined. After the resurrection, the body will no longer require sustenance; therefore, the motions of the heavenly bodies will cease; and animals, plants, and all compound substances will be resolved into their elements, purged by fire, and clothed in new and glorious brightness; and we shall be forever happy with the Lord,

CHAPTER VI.

THE DOCTRINE OF THE DAMNATION OF THE WICKED IS ONE BEFITTING CHRISTIANITY.

As the just deserve the glory of Heaven, the wicked, who have gone aside from God, deserve the lowest place on earth, wherein they and their sins may be punished. There is no injustice in the eternity of punishment inflicted for temporal guilt. Even human law (as in the case of death or lifelong exile), avenges certain crimes by unending punishment. The wicked are justly deprived for all eternity of glory, and punished forever in hell — not for their passing sins so much as for the malice of their will, which remained obstinately inclined to sin until death. Surely, is it not most reasonable to believe, that they who have preferred temporal pleasure to eternal glory, and would, (had it been possible), have persevered in this choice, should be punished with eternal suffering; the more so as, after this life, they are no longer capable of meriting eternal life? Again, as we have already remarked, it is not the soul alone, but the whole man who acts, and if it be reasonable that the just should be glorified in soul and body, the wicked equally deserve twofold punishment.

There are in hell other torments besides that of fire. But because fire is the most active it is always spoken of as the chief punishment. The bodies of the damned are not consumed by this fire, for the Divine Power enables their souls to preserve these bodies from destruction. But as, by malice, these souls have turned away from their Creator, their bodies are not perfectly subject to them; they are therefore capable of suffering excruciating torments in the fire of hell, though not of being consumed by it.

CHAPTER VII.

THE DOCTRINE OF THE INCARNATION OF THE SON OF GOD IS, IN NO SENSE, INCREDIBLE, UNSEEMLY, OR UNREASONABLE.

The Christian religion maintains inviolably that God is that His person subsists in two natures, viz., the Divine Nature and the Human; and that the union between these natures is so perfect that the Person who is God is likewise Man. No parallel to this union can be found in nature, for the simple reason, that no perfect created substance can be united to another substance in such a manner as to become one with it. Even the union between soul and body cannot be compared to the union between the Word and the human nature. The soul is the form of the body; but form is imperfect; and as God is Perfection, the Word cannot be the form of the human nature. Moreover, the Divine Nature and the human are in Christ two perfect substances; and therefore the union between them surpasses understanding. We must not, however, say that this union is impossible. God can do many things beyond the capacity of our intelligence. Then, in the union between the Divine and Human nature. His Divine Majesty suffers no change; but human nature is, by His infinite power, raised to wondrous union with His Person.

Neither can we call this union unseemly or unreasonable. For, from it countless blessings have come to the world, benefits so numerous indeed that we could not attempt to name them all, but must content ourselves with recounting some of them.

First. The Incarnation has been a most powerful

means, whereby man ma^ attain happiness. The true beatitude of man consists, as we know, in the vision of the Divine Essence. But, considering the limitations of human intelligence, and the sublimity of the Divine Nature, we might justly have despaired of gaining this supreme happiness. Therefore, God, by uniting in His own Person the Divine with the Human Nature, (a union far surpassing the union between the Divine Essence and the understanding of the blessed), has willed to hold forth to man hopes of attaining to the glory for which he was created. And man, since the Incarnation, has aspired to happiness, with greater ardor than he did before this mystery was accomplished.

Again. The Incarnation, wherein God has united Himself (directly, without intermediary), to man,... has made clear to man that God is His sole End, and has thus taught him to appreciate the excellence of his own nature. It has so far enlightened the human race, that men, at the sight of this wonderful union between God and man, have abandoned the worship of idols. Then, in their quest of true religion and unalloyed happiness, they have despised all earthly wealth and dignity and pleasure.

We must further remember that, as the happiness, whereunto we were created, far exceeds the capacity of our understanding, it would have been impossible for us to have had any sure knowledge or hope of it. Even the investigations instituted by the most learned philosophers would have been in vain. Befitting therefore was it, that God, in His special Providence over man, should take flesh, in order to assure man of his future blessedness and to confirm his hopes of it. Hence, by the Incarnation, mankind has a far more complete and clear knowledge of beatitude and of Divine things.

We know, likewise, that man, before the Incarnation, was entangled in affection for many temporal things. By His Incarnation, God took the surest means possible to raise him from earth to the love of eternal things. For, who, seeing this great love of God towards man, will not be moved to love Him in return? And, in fact, since God's love for man has been known upon earth, men have been so much inflamed with desire for Divine things, that they have entered into friendship with God, and with His saints; and they have despised all earthly ties.

Again. Certain means are necessary to enable man to gain happiness. These means are virtue and spiritual perfection. These graces have, by the Incarnation, been abundantly poured out upon mankind. The proof of this lies in the fact that, since the coming of Christ, the world has been so fertile in examples of virtue and perfection, that none, save the blind, can doubt that the teaching of Christ is the one sure road to blessedness. Thus, we see, that the Catholic faith teaches, in the dogma of the Incarnation, nothing either incredible or unreasonable.

CHAPTER VIII.

THE BELIEF IN THE VIRGINAL BIRTH OF CHRIST IS CONSISTENT WITH REASON, AND HIS LIFE BEFITTED, IN ALL RESPECTS, HIS DIGNITY.

Hitherto we have undertaken to prove the credibility and congruity of our belief in the more difficult articles of the Christian creed. We will now proceed to discuss such as are easier. First then, if God was able to become Man, He was also able to be born of a virgin. For generation signifies the" production of a person, not of a nature; and birth means the entrance into the world, not of human nature, but of an individual man or woman, subsisting in that nature. Now, as the Person of the Son of God subsisted in human nature, it was possible for God to be born of a woman, from whom He took that nature. God might, certainly, have formed the body of Christ from the earth, or from some other material. He might have done so; but He did not, because it was more fitting that it should have been born of a woman, in order that the sight of the Father of all things deigning to have an earthly mother and kinsfolk and country, and to suffer the infirmities of human life for love of us, should excite us to deeper humility.

It was, likewise, most seemly that He who in Heaven had no mother, and whose Father was the God of all Purity, should choose for His earthly mother a spotless virgin, and that He should have no earthly father. 20

It was, moreover, highly fitting that Christ should not have lived a solitary life, but should have mingled with men. For since He had come upon earth, in order, by His preaching, to induce mankind to seek for eternal happiness, it was necessary that He should not, like St. John the Baptist', lead an austere life but an ordinary one; that He should follow, in His eating, drinking, and other habits of life, the customs of His country; that thus He might enable men to profit by His words and example. Neither, by choosing the common life, did He in any sense contravene the principles of the spiritual life. For, perfection does not necessarily consist in austerity, but in sincerity and ardent charity; which, by fixing our mind on eternal things, ensures us against elation in prosperity, and depression in adversity.

It was also most fitting that Christ should, by His poverty, set an example to preachers, showing them that they ought to be free from solicitude about earthly gains, and from the least taint of avarice. The poverty of Christ, likewise, threw into stronger relief the power of His Divine Majesty, which alone, unaided by worldly power or learning, sufficed to transform the world. His miracles, again, are reasonably to be expected, since it was by them that He manifested His Divinity. Finally, if we reverently and humbly study all His words and works, we shall find in them the most admirable sequence, and most perfect order.

CHAPTER IX.

THE CHRISTIAN DOCTRINE OF ORIGINAL SIN IS NEITHER UNREASONABLE NOR INCREDIBLE.

In order the better to understand both what has been said, and what still remains to be said, we must touch on the subject of that original sin, whereby the whole human race has been defiled. We have already shown, that God, in His own good time, created the world, placing over it, as the head of all things, man, endowed with an intellectual, immortal and most noble soul; and that to this soul was fitted an immortal body, obedient in all things and proportioned to the soul, which, as form, governs its matter, the body. But, since intellectual knowledge depends upon the senses, and senses cannot have any being save in a body composed of fleshly elements warring against reason, the only body that befits the soul is the human body.

Nevertheless, we believe, with good reason, that Divine Providence, which never fails His creatures, mercifully delivered man at his creation, from corruption, and from that repugnance to reason inherent in the flesh; and that He so proportioned the matter of the body to its form, the soul, that the inferior powers were subject to reason. Hence, we say that man was, at his creation, endowed with original justice, i.e., with impassibility, and subjection of body to soul, and of the sensitive part of his nature to reason. We further hold that this original justice would, had not Adam deliberately disobeyed God, have descended to all his posterity. But is most reasonable, that, if man willfully chose to turn aside from God, he should be deprived of original justice, of the natural subjection of his senses to reason, and of the immortality of his body. This was the just punishment of his sin. This deprivation of original justice, inflicted On Adam, and transmitted by him to the whole human race, is what we mean by original sin.

We see in man such evident proofs of the truth of this doctrine, that it appeals strongly to our reason. The Providence of God rewards good deeds, and punishes evil ones. When we see a penalty inflicted, we know that some fault has preceded it. Now, we behold the human body subject to many sufferings — to cold and heat, to hunger and thirst, to sickness and to death. We see, moreover, that the intellectual soul is weak in reason and in will; that it is harassed by the flesh; and, that, by reason of these infirmities, man falls, daily, into many errors. These sufferings are the sign of some antecedent fault. But, although the deficiencies of man seem proper to his nature, God could have supplied them all, had not man, by his own fault, placed an obstacle in the way. Therefore, it is quite reasonable to say, that the defects in human nature, are the outcome of the sin of our first parent, the representative of our whole race.

The sin of Adam was at the same time both personal and common to all nature. It was personal, in so far as it deprived Adam of original justice. It was common, in so far as the deprivation extended to all his posterity. From the point of view of the will of the human race, this privation does not imply sin; but from the point of view of the malice of Adam, this subtraction of original justice is the direct consequence of his sin. And, as he is our head and we are his members, he has implicated us in his guilt. The actual taking of a thing unjustly with the hand is thieving, and is called sin : yet the sin is not in the hand, but in the malice of him that moves the hand to steal. In like manner our privation of original justice would not be accounted unto us for sin, nor should we be born in sin, had we not been, by our first parent, implicated in his sin. His malice has affected all the members of his body, and therefore we, who are his members, are all born in original sin. But if Adam had never been endowed with original justice, and consequently had never lost it, we, had we been born with the irregularity now existent in our nature, should not have been born in sin. Ours would have been a purely natural state. For, where there is no malice in the will, there cannot be sin. It is, therefore, the malice of our first parent which causes the privation of original justice, transmitted by him to the human race, to be accounted as original sin.

There is nothing unjust in the fact that all men have to suffer the penalty due to one. Man had no natural right to original justice, in the sense in which he has a right to the use of his limbs. Justice was a free gift of God; and the giver has power to choose the time, and manner, of his gift. If God gave to Adam original justice, with the understanding that if he did not sin, both he and all his posterity should keep this gift; but that if he did sin, both he and his descendants should be deprived of their privilege, what ground have we for complaint? Human nature, in its entirety, was included in Adam. Since then, original justice is, in no sense, our due, we could not murmur had Adam never been graced with it. How therefore can we complain that, in consequence of Adam's violation of the conditions imposed Upon him by God, our nature has been deprived of this privilege? Original sin does not, as is often thought, mean simply a wound inflicted on human nature, which has injured it by depriving it of some good proper to it. It means, rather, the deprivation, of that state original

151

justice, to which human nature has no claim. It is as unreasonable to murmur at being born in our purely natural state, as it would be to complain that we were not sanctified in the womb, or were not created in the enjoyment of happiness.

Man cannot attain to beatitude without the gift of supernatural grace. Therefore, he who dies in original sin is deprived of eternal life; but he is not, therefore and thereby, subjected to any sorrow or suffering. Not being proportioned to beatitude, he is incapable of enjoying it. He does not, however, suffer from the loss; because God rectifies his will, conforming it to His own, and taking from it the desire of that which is impossible to it. A man who has no claim to an imperial crown, does not grieve because he is not an Emperor. Neither does such a soul suffer any sensible pain. On the contrary, it is endowed with all perfection proper to
human nature — such as the knowledge of all natural things, and even the contemplation, by means of creatures, of such as are Divine. It enjoys all the happiness which human nature can enjoy. Furthermore, God confers upon these souls certain supernatural gifts — such as immortality, and impassibility of body — so that they are not subject to human infirmity; nor will they ever suffer sensible pain. And, although we believe that the abode of these souls is Limbo, the place of their habitation signifies but little. My private opinion, (subject to any future pronouncement of the Holy Roman Church), is, that after the resurrection, they will dwell on the purified and glorified earth. My reason for thus thinking is, that if the place of habitation be proportioned to the inhabitant, souls informing immortal and impassible bodies, and enjoying all the happiness natural to man, ought not to be deprived of the light of the sun and of other natural advantages and

delights, in which they could have no share were they detained in a subterranean Limbo. We may go further, and say, that such a deprivation would not only be a diminution of happiness, but a sensible pain. Original sin, however, although it involves, as its consequence, the loss of the Beatific Vision, does not imply the endurance of sensible pain. Thus, we see, that God, in His dealings with souls that pass from life in original sin, manifests, in a peculiar manner. His justice and His wisdom. We see also that the Christian teaching concerning original sin is neither incredible nor unreasonable.

CHAPTER X.

OUR BELIEF IN THE PASSION OF CHRIST, IN THE OTHER MYSTERIES OF HIS HUMANITY, AND IN ALL THE ARTICLES DEFINED BY THE CHURCH, IS STRICTLY CONSISTENT WITH REASON.

God, the Father of mercies, who is all bountiful, has supplied for the defects caused by original sin, certain fitting remedies. Of these the chief are: first, the faith and sacrifices of the Patriarchs; next, Circumcision; and thirdly, Holy Baptism. These remedies render man capable of attaining, by grace, to supernatural happiness.

And if we do not receive this grace, we ought to blame, not the Providence of God, but the remissness of our parents.

Some persons may find a difficulty in the fact, that, although the Saints of the Old Testament died in a state of grace and cleansed from original sin, they nevertheless were debarred from entering Heaven. The answer to this objection is, that, as original sin was an offence against God, imputed, not to individuals, but to human nature, it was necessary that His Divine Majesty should be satisfied, before the gates of Paradise could be opened. And again, as, by original sin, guilt was incurred by human nature, which may be said to be composed of an infinite number of persons, this guilt was in a manner infinite, and demanded satisfaction, not from one individual alone, since every creature is finite, but from the whole human race.

But, another difficulty may be raised on this point. It may be argued, that it beseems the infinite mercy of God to accept from man the satisfaction which he is capable of making, and to remit the debt which he cannot pay. We answer, that, had there been no other possibility of satisfying for original sin, God would have accepted the only satisfaction which man was capable of making. But, as He was able to satisfy His justice by other means. He chose to make use of these other means, thereby both satisfying for sin, and perfecting human nature. Man could not, of himself, atone for sin. Only God, who has never sinned, "could make fitting satisfaction for it. Therefore, He, in His infinite mercy, wisdom, and power, willed, by becoming man, to pay the debt which man owed, and was unable to pay.

Man owed satisfaction, and God-made Man, alone had power to make that satisfaction, not, indeed, for Himself, but for the whole human race. In this fact is revealed the fitness of His Incarnation, wherein He has united the Divine to the Human nature. In this mystery we behold His power. His wisdom, and the goodness whereby He has wholly given Himself to the human race, to embrace it, and draw it to His love. But, above all His other attributes, His mercy is made manifest; for it has led Him to be crucified for love of us. His justice also is seen; for He has Himself made satisfaction for original sin. Hence, while His mercy should inspire repentant sinners with the surest hope, His Justice should cause the impenitent to tremble. This is the reason why, since the coming of Christ into the world, so many men have been drawn from sin to holiness of life.

When we consider these mercies, and the innumerable other benefits conferred by Christ upon human nature, we discover depths of wisdom which are unfathomable by the intellect of man, and which, for this very reason, are accounted folly by the world. We see, moreover, how fitting it was that Christ should suffer for the guilt of mankind.

But since He came, not merely to suffer for man, but likewise to set him an example of righteous living, it behoved Him to choose a most bitter and disgraceful death; thus teaching us that neither shame, nor suffering, should force us to betray the cause of truth and justice. Time forbids me to enlarge upon the other reasons which caused our Saviour to choose His terrible mode of death, I will only add, that His cross has been, to them that love Him, a fount of sweetness and of light, known only to those who have experienced it.

As Christ died in order to make satisfaction for our sins, and especially for that original sin, on account of which the Patriarchs were detained in Limbo, it was meet that, being already delivered from original sin, they should be enlightened by the descent of Christ into Limbo, which took place immediately after His death. And it was, likewise, most fitting that he should remain for three days in the tomb. Had He stayed there longer, men would have lost all hope of His Resurrection; and had He not remained in the sepulchre so long, they would have denied the reality of His death. But, as abode in this present life does not befit the life of glory, Christ, after His Resurrection, did' not converse with men, as He had done before His death. But, as His body was perfect, and noble above all human bodies, on account both of the perfection of His Soul, and of His union with the Word, He ascended into Heaven and sits at the right hand of the Father, as His true and sole-begotten Son. The expression sits at the right hand of the Father, is not to be understood as referring to bodily posture, but as signifying that Christ, beyond all creatures, enjoyed the fruition of eternal happiness. And, if it be asked how

His body could penetrate the heavens, we answer that the Divine Power can enable two bodies to exist together.

Further, it is fitting that the Son of God, who was unjustly judged by men, should be the Head, and Standard, and Judge of the living and the dead. For, in this wise, does His reward correspond to the suffering which He bore for us. Thus, if we reflect, we shall see that the acts which Christ performed in the world are full of mysteries; and we shall understand, that the Christian religion is not only reasonable, but wonderful, and Divine.

We have already spoken of the faith which enables us to believe everything contained in Holy Scripture; and we have shown how true it is and how reasonable. We have also shown, that, as the objects of our faith can proceed from no one but from God, we are bound to believe them unwaveringly. But since, in doctrine as in material things, every movable thing must be reduced to something immovable, we acknowledge, with the fullest reason, that God has established in His Church, over which He exercises peculiar care, certain unchanging doctrines to which all men must submit, doctrines which contain those first principles from which all conclusions are deduced. Therefore, the Catholic Faith most fittingly holds, that all that the Holy Roman Church has defined, or shall define, is most certain truth. It rejects all other teaching. For the Church, as we shall show hereafter, is the firm and solid foundation of the faith, and our guide to salvation.

CHAPTER XI.

THE CHRISTIAN RELIGION MOST PRUDENTLY ESTABLISHES THE TWO PRECEPTS OF CHARITY. AS THE FOUNDATION OF OUR WHOLE MORAL LIFE.

We have already shown, that the Christian religion teaches nothing concerning faith which is either impossible or irrational. We shall now proceed to prove that this is likewise the case in those matters which regard morals. And, although we have already given sufficient proofs of this fact, when we pointed out that the Christian life is the best life possible; nevertheless, as things are better understood in particular than in general, we will descend to some details.

The first principle and foundation of our moral doctrine is the commandment, "They shalt love the Lord thy God with thy whole heart, with thy whole soul, with all thy mind, and with all thy strength"(Deut. 6:5; Matt. 22:37; Mark 12:30; Luke 10:27).

And the second commandment is, "Thou shalt love thy neighbor as thyself"(Lev. 19:18; Matt. 22:39; Mark 12:31; Luke 10:37). We must not understand these commandments as meaning that it is sufficient for salvation to love God and our neighbor from natural virtue or inclination. Our love must proceed from supernatural grace, for the reception of which we must diligently prepare ourselves. Thus, the first principle and foundation of the Christian moral life, is the obligation to love God, by means of supernatural charity, more than ourselves; and to order ourselves and all things else to His glory, as to our end. St. Paul expresses this precept in the following words, "Whether you eat or drink, or whatsoever else you do, do all to the glory of God"(1 Cor. 10:31).

But since the rebelliousness of the flesh withdraws men greatly from the love of God, the precept adds, "thou shalt love the Lord thy God with thy whole heart," which signifies, thou shalt love Him in such a way that thou shalt subjugate thy sensitive affections to thy will. For by the heart, is here meant, those sensibilities of our nature which are the fount and source of desires which separate us from Divine love. And since the will goes astray, if it be not conformed to reason, the commandment adds the words, "and with thy whole soul," whereby we understand the will. For, since the soul is in animals the principle of life and motion, whereby we distinguish animate from inanimate beings, so, likewise, does the will move all the powers of the rational soul. Therefore, God commands us to love Him with our whole will; so that all our activities may be directed to Him; our love, desire, joy, fear, and hope, may all be centered on Him; and our whole soul may turn, in horror, from all that is contrary to His will, or derogatory to His honour. The inclination of the will depends entirely on reason; for we cannot desire what we do not know. This is expressed by the words in the commandment, "with thy whole mind, "by which is meant our understanding and our reason. These must be turned to God, who must, either habitually or actually, be the chief object of our contemplation. But we are bound to honour God, not only with our souls, but with our bodies, working our external works to His glory. Therefore, the commandment concludes with the words, "all thy strength". Observe the word all, remembering that an end, being loved for itself, is not loved according to measure; but the means, being ordained to an end, are loved in proportion to the end to which they are ordered.

Since, then, God is our End, we are commanded to love Him with our whole heart, with our whole soul, with all our mind, and all our strength. That is to say, that, both interiorly and exteriorly, we must be wholly directed to God, and lead perfect lives; so that in us God may be glorified, as the Cause is honoured by the perfection of its effect. This commandment teaches us, further, in what manner man is bound to love himself. For self-love must be directed to God, who must be glorified in man, as in His own work.

But, as the love of others is not so natural to man as is self-love, we are taught how we must love our neigh-bour by the words, "thou shalt love thy neighbor as thyself". That is, thy love of others shall be governed by the same motive as that which directs thy love of thyself; and thou must desire for thy neighbor that same perfection of life, and the other blessings, which thou do desire for thyself; so that in him, God may be honoured and glorified, as in His most perfect work. Nothing, surely, can be conceived more reasonable, than these two commandments, on which depend all other laws, both human and Divine. Therefore all that is included in them, or results from them, is by Christians esteemed holy and inviolable; and whatever impugns them, is reputed impious and diabolical.

CHAPTER XII.

THE EXCELLENCE OF THE MORAL TEACHING OF THE CHURCH.

We have already shown how reasonably Holy Scripture sets before us two tables of commandments: one teaching us our duty to God, and the other showing what we owe to our neighbor. For, as each man forms part of a community, he must be rightly disposed, both towards the head of the community, and to his fellow-members; that is to say, towards God, and towards his neighbors. Man is rightly disposed towards God, when He loves Him with his whole heart, his whole soul, with all his mind, and with all his strength. But as we owe to our civil rulers three duties, viz., loyalty, reverence, and obedient service, the Christian religion sums up these our obligations to God in three commandments. The first commandment bids us to honour the one only true God, and none other: the second, to reverence His Holy Name; the third, to pay Him obedient service, by honouring His day, by both interior and exterior acts of worship. From these three commandments spring all the other precepts which relate to man's service of God; and by disobedience to them, he forfeits his eternal salvation.

The second table of the Law concerns man's duty to his neighbor. This consists in doing him good, and avoiding injury to him. The first commandment of this table is, "Honour thy father and thy mother". And the honour which we are hereby bidden to render to our parents means, not merely that we must reverence them in our words, but, likewise, that we must help them by good works. The next three commandments forbid us to injure any one. We can do harm to others in three ways, namely by injury to them in their own person; by injuring them in the person of those connected with them; and by injuring their property. Hence, the first of these commandments forbids homicide, The second prohibits adultery; and the third theft. And, as we are commanded to abstain from injury to others, not only in deed, but also in word or desire, the next commandment forbids false testimony; and the two following warn us against coveting either the wife, or the property of another.

But, it may be asked, why are only these two par-ticular forms of covetousness specified, when desires contrary to any of the other commandments are equally criminal? I answer, that the evangelical law punishes, not only exterior deeds, but likewise interior inordinate affections. Special mention has, however, been made of these two kinds of evil desire, because men might hesitate to condemn them; whereas they would consider interior rebellion against God or infidelity to Him in-excusable; and they would look on contempt of parents, or desire to bring death or dishonor on their fellow-men as equally detestable. But a covetous longing for the property of others seems so natural to man, that unless such covetousness had been expressly forbidden, he would not have regarded it as sinful. We see, therefore, how perfectly Christianity legislates for mankind in all things, whether internal or external; "and that all other precepts, and all philosophical systems of ethics, may be reduced to these ten commandments, which, in fact, comprise points which no heathen sages have ever understood.

Certain counsels are, furthermore, subjoined to the

commandments. For, as the whole scope of the Christian life tends to the perfection of Divine love, which cannot be attained without purity of heart, the teaching of the Church divides the Christian law into two parts, namely, into positive and negative laws and precepts. The positive laws regard the perfection of charity by enjoining good works. The negative precepts concern purity, by forbidding all that can defile the soul. Now, in order to complete the perfection of this charity and purity, Christ has left us certain counsels. He exhorts those that will be perfect, to sell all that they have and give it to the poor; to observe chastity; and to embrace the religious life, whereby they will renounce not only earthly possessions, but themselves, in order to become entirely devoted to the contemplation of eternal things, and, in a certain sense, to be made one with God. In these counsels, we behold the consummate wisdom of the Christian religion, in all matters pertaining to morality. For nothing, required by reason, is neglected; and nothing contrary to reason is enjoined. A comparison of this system with any other school of ethics, will show a superiority, as marked as is the distance between heaven and earth, or the difference between light and darkness.

CHAPTER XIII.

THE PERFECT REASONABLENESS OF THE CHRISTIAN CONSTITUTION AND CODE OF JUDICIAL LAW.

The Christian judicial system, furthermore, can be proved to be highly reasonable. For, as in every process there is some principle, which is the measure of other things, there must be in law some principle or standard which is the Eternal Law, or certain rule of Divine Wisdom, governing all the operations and motions of creatures. From this law all other laws , take their rise; for the power of the first motor is felt by all inferior motors.

This rule and standard exists in God, as in the Supreme Ruler, and in creatures as in things governed and set in motion by Him, subject to His Providence, and impressed with the character of His law, which inclines them to their proper end.

Rational creatures, being subject, in a peculiar manner, to Divine Providence, are also, in a special way, governed by this law; and their obedience to this Divine law renders it necessary that they should be ruled, likewise, by a certain natural law. Now, the origin of this natural law is the light of reason, impressed by God on man making clear to him certain principles, both in practical and in speculative matters. These principles are known as first or natural laws. From these first laws all other laws are deduced. And they are deduced in one of two ways, viz., as conclusions drawn from manifest principles, (as is generally the case in speculative science); or as axioms laid down and approved by prudent men, as is the case with artists who formulate general rules, to be applied in particular cases. Thus, an

architect, in erecting an individual building, will follow certain principles, universally observed in all architecture. In matters concerning morals, law is administered by means either of conclusions drawn from universal natural laws: e.g., murder is forbidden; to poison another is to murder him; therefore, giving poison to others is forbidden. Or else, the law is applied by means of certain definite rules, laid down by legislators, applying the universal natural law to particular cases. For instance there is a general law declaring that crime must be punished; but the particular penalty to be inflicted for a particular crime must be determined by the judgment of prudent men, and for the common good. Such laws must, evidently, vary according to circumstances. These are called positive, or human, laws. We see, at once, that all men are not governed by these differing positive laws; whereas the natural laws are invariable and binding on all races. They are binding, not merely insofar as they are general principles, but likewise in the case of
the particular laws deduced from these general principles.

For true principles cannot give rise to false conclusions. But, as natural law would not suffice for the government of human life, the assistance of the Divine law is also necessary; and this for several reasons.

First, because, by law man is directed to the attainment of his last end; but, as his last end is supernatural, natural law would not suffice to guide him to it.

Secondly, our understanding is so feeble, that, the more we descend to particulars, the greater difficulty we experience in judging aright. The Divine law is therefore necessary, to enable us to arrive at just conclusions in particular cases.

Thirdly, human law does not punish or forbid every-thing that is criminal; it allows many lesser evils in order to ward off greater ones. Therefore, a law was necessary, which should show man that guilt, unpunished by human law, would be avenged by Divine law.

Fourthly human law judges not the hidden things of the heart, but only exterior actions. Therefore, in order to teach us that we must be perfect both interiorly and exteriorly, the Divine law, which punishes the sins of the heart, was necessary.

This Divine law may be called a compendium of the Divine commandments, and it proceeds from the light of Faith. We, therefore, speak of it as being essentially the grace of the Holy Spirit, from which spring all the commandments of which we have spoken. And from these universal precepts are deduced, (either by conclusion or by specially formulated axioms), all particular laws. The particular laws, derived from the Divine Law, are called canonical laws. Those deduced from natural law are termed civil laws. The laity are governed by civil, and the clergy by canonical law.

There is no opposition between the Divine and the natural law. But, as grace perfects nature, the Divine law perfects the natural law; and all that pertains to the natural law pertains, likewise, to the Divine law.

The moral teaching of our natural reason is said to belong to the natural law. The duties imposed on us by the light of grace are called the precepts of the Divine law. We must not, however, imagine that everything that is contained in the Divine law belongs to the natural law; for the Sacraments and the truths of Faith pertain, solely, to the Divine, and not to the natural law. The Christian religion, then, is organized by the Divine law. It excludes nothing which is in accordance with truth or morality; it admits nothing contrary to them.

Therefore, as Christians, we do not despise the good and reasonable laws, of either uncivilized nations, or of heathen philosophers. On the contrary, we select from those laws all that is true and virtuous, and ascribe it to God, who, for the sake of His elect, has created all truth and all goodness.

On the other hand, our religion is so averse to all fables or falsehood, that it will not authorize even such books as have been written to glorify the Faith and the deeds of the Saints, unless the author be reliable, and the truth of his writing manifest. And, if, in the government of the Church, some unjust law exist, it exists, not through the fault of the Christian religion, but, by reason of the impiety of some tyrant, whom the Church condemns and execrates. Thus, we see, that the Christian religion is most reasonably administered, by means both of civil and of Divine laws.

CHAPTER XIV.

THE SACRAMENTS OF THE CHURCH HAVE BEEN INSTITUTED BY CHRIST, AND ARE ADMIRABLY ADAPTED TO THE NEEDS OF MANKIND.

It is our intention to treat, in this chapter, of the ceremonies of the Church. And, as her Sacraments are the chief ceremonies — all other rights being ordained on their account — we will begin by proving how absolutely reasonable these Sacraments are. And thus, all the other rites of the Church will be more easily understood. Christ, by His Passion, is the universal cause of our salvation. But, just as, in the law of nature, a universal cause "only operates by means of particular causes, which apply its virtue to particular effects, it is likewise most reasonable that there should be some particular cause of our salvation, whereby the virtue of the Passion of Christ should be applied to our souls. This particular cause is found in the Sacraments of the Church, which are the channels of Christ's grace to the soul. And, as a particular cause must be proportioned to the universal cause, and an instrument to the agent; it is most reasonable and fitting, that the Sacraments should be composed of external signs and of words, thus representing Christ, the Word of the Eternal Father united to human nature. And, since none can be saved without grace, we can say most truly, that these Sacraments are Christ's instruments in the conferring of grace. We do not mean, that their power is able to produce the final effect of grace; but we speak in the sense used by philosophers, when they say that man is begotten of man and of the sun's heat; not meaning, of course, that either human or solar power is capable of producing the intellectual soul of man. We must remember that an instrument acts in two ways; first, by its own form, as in the case of a saw, which from the metal of which it is made and its serrated shape, is able to cut wood; secondly, by the power and movement of the agent, which, as in the case of the carpenter using a saw, gives a specific form to the wood. But, this power does not always produce the ultimate effect on that on which it is exercised. For we see, that, though creatures are the instruments used by God in human generation, they do not beget the intellectual soul of man, which is created immediately by God; but that they are only instrumental in the final disposition of matter, and in the union of soul with body. In the same way, the Sacraments are not, either by their own virtue, or by power acquired from the movement of Christ, the chief agent, able to produce their final effect, which is grace. Grace proceeds from God alone; but the Sacraments dispose the soul for the reception of grace; and this disposition, imparted by them, is, by theologians, called their character.

We see a proof that the Sacraments thus confer grace, in the good life of those who receive them, in their con- version from vice to virtue, and in the progress in perfection made by those who frequent them. As we have, however, in the preceding Book, treated at length of these effects, we will say no more about them for the present.

CHAPTER XV.

THE NUMBER OF THE SACRAMENTS IS REASONABLE.

Since Christ is the universal cause of our salvation and of the spiritual life by which we live to God; and since we understand spiritual things by the likeness which they bear to such as are physical; we must distinguish the Sacraments which are instituted for the spiritual life, by comparing them with those things which are ordained for corporeal life.

Now, in physical life, we have : first, generation, whereby life is acquired; secondly, development, whereby the body is perfected; thirdly, nutrition, whereby it is preserved. Thus the vegetative life possesses powers of generation, of growth, and of nutrition. But for the animal nature, as sickness may attack it, nature provides fitting remedies; and as generation cannot occur without a parent, some generating factor must exist in the world. Corresponding to these needs of the physical life, we have in the spiritual life many Sacraments. Of these the first is Baptism, whereby man is born again in Christ.

The second is Confirmation, whereby grace is increased within him, and he is rendered strong enough to endure the trials, through which all must pass on their way to eternal life.

The third is the Blessed Eucharist, without which the spiritual life of man would flag, as his body would faint without food.

The fourth is the Sacrament of Penance, whereby he

recovers spiritual health, and the wounds of his soul are healed.

The fifth is Extreme Unction, which heals the soul, and, (since bodily sickness is sometimes caused by sin), in some cases restores health to the body; or, when recover)' from sickness is not expedient, it enables the soul to pass, more devoutly and easily, to eternal life.

The sixth Sacrament is that of Holy Orders, which provides fathers for the spiritual life.

Then, since the spiritual life could not endure, were the human race to be extinct, we have the Sacrament of Matrimony, which is the seventh Sacrament of the Church. Thus we see, that, as in the physical order the propagators of physical life may be regarded, either as the principles of the life of their progeny, or as the rulers and superiors of their children, so in the spiritual order, Christ has ordained seven Sacraments to be the principles and the organizers of the spiritual life.

We see, then, how wisely, and how advisedly, Christ has instituted seven Sacraments in His Church.

CHAPTER XVI.

THE RITES USED IN THE ADMINISTRATION OF THE SACRAMENTS ARE BOTH REASONABLE AND SEEMLY.

The matter and symbols, used in the administration of our Sacraments, are likewise most fittingly ordained. Let us first consider Baptism, the Sacrament of re-generation. We know that birth signifies the change from non-being into being; and that as all men are born in original sin, they are all born in a state of privation of grace or spiritual life; and in proportion as they add actual to original sin, they are still further deprived of grace. Therefore, it was most meet, that Christ should give to the Sacrament of Baptism power to remit sin, and to confer grace and spiritual life. Again, as bodily stains are effaced by water, it was fitting that water should be chosen as the matter of this Sacrament. And, as we can be born but once, it is reasonable that Baptism can be but once conferred.

The perfection of spiritual life consists in a constant and courageous confession of the Cross of Christ, and in boldly enduring insult for His sake. In order to produce in us this effect, He has instituted the Sacrament of Confirmation. Those who fight under a commander, bear upon them his device or crest; and so those who receive Confirmation are signed on the forehead with the Cross, in order to show, that they must not be ashamed to be the soldiers of Christ. This Cross is made of oil and of balsam. The oil signifies that the conscience of him that is anointed must shine, like oil, with those gifts of the Holy Ghost, wherewith Jesus being most excellently endowed, was called Christ, or anointed. The ^balsam symbolizes the sweet odor of virtue, which Christians are bound to diffuse around them. It is fitting, likewise, that bishops alone should be empowered to administer this Sacrament, since they are the leaders of the army of Christ; and the captains of an army alone can adorn their soldiers with their insignia.

The Blessed Eucharist being ordained for the nourishment of the spiritual life, it is meet that its outward signs should be bread and wine. And, as food is substantially joined to the body which is nourished, we believe that Christ exists in this Sacrament, not only by His power, but in His substance; and that He is thus present, in order to unite Himself so intimately with them that receive Him with faith and love, as to become one with them. Furthermore, as the Blessed Eucharist is to be a memorial of His Passion, wherein His Body and Blood were divided, it is meet that His body should be given to us under the appearance of bread, and His Blood under the form of wine; although Christ Himself is wholly present in each species.

When we consider the Sacrament of penance, we must remember that physical health proceeds, sometimes, from natural strength of constitution, and, sometimes, from the assistance of a physician and of remedies. The same thing holds good in the spiritual order, but with certain limitations. For the health of the soul cannot proceed entirely from our intrinsic power — none being able to deliver himself from sin without grace; neither can it be altogether effected by extrinsic assistance — for the co-operation of our will is always required. Spiritual health, therefore, needs both an exterior, and an interior, agent. And, as we call a man physically sound, when he is free from all weakness caused by disease, we say, in like manner, that the soul is healed, when it is freed from all the infirmity caused by sin. Now, sin produces three bad effects. The first of these is aversion of the soul from God, and its conversion to creatures. The second is the penalty incurred by its guilt And the third is a diminution of grace and weakness of will; for, by sin, the soul becomes more prone to evil, and more disinclined to good. Therefore, the remedial Sacrament of Penance is most reasonably ordained to remedy these three evils. The first part of this Sacrament is contrition, which delivers the soul from aversion to God, causing it to repent of sin and to return to its Maker; frees it from the penalty of eternal death, which cannot remain due to a soul in grace and charity; and renders it inclined to good and averse to evil. But, as contrition is not perfect in all men, it does not always remit the entire penalty of sin. The Lord has, therefore, added two other parts to the Sacrament of Penance, -to wit, Confession . and Satisfaction. Man may wish to pay in this life the penalty which remains due to him after contrition; but he cannot know what this penalty may be; he must therefore submit himself to the judgment of Christ, to whom alone he owes satisfaction. But, as Christ, glorified in Heaven, is to us invisible. He has left in His place, as His ministers, the priests of the Church.

A judge cannot, however, assess the penalty, if he be ignorant of the crime. Therefore a sinner must make confession to a priest. This confession is the second part of the Sacrament of Penance. It follows, that the ministers of Christ, in their judicial capacity, must be invested with a twofold power. First, they must be invested with authority and knowledge to judge the gravity of sin. Secondly, they must have ability to bind and to loose. This power of binding and loosing is known as the power of the Keys. Now, as the Sacraments are the instruments of grace, it is quite certain, that, by this power of the Keys, a penitent obtains more grace, and fuller remission of punishment, than he could receive merely by contrition. It sometimes happens, however, that contrition and confession do not suffice to remit the entire penalty incurred by sin. Therefore, a third part has been added to the Sacrament of Penance, namely Satisfaction, or the performance of a penance enjoined by the priest.

The Sacrament of Extreme Unction has been most fittingly ordained by Christ, in consideration of human weakness. For, as bodily sickness is often both the effect of sin, and the cause of grave spiritual detriment, a Sacrament was necessary which should repair this detriment, and should heal both soul and body; or should, at least, enable the soul to pass more easily, and with greater purity, into the other life. For the Sacrament of Penance does not always remit the entire penalty due to sin; nor does it wholly remove all inclination to sin and slothfulness in the performance of good. Nay, these evils are oftentimes increased in sickness, by pain and anxiety of mind, which hinder the dying from the remembrance of their sins. Thus, at the hour of death, there may be many remnants of sin in the soul, which call for powerful assistance, to enable a man to depart, purified, to eternal glory. Now, this assistance is given by that Sacrament, which — to denote that it should only be administered in sickness unto death — we call Extreme Unction. The matter of this Sacrament is oil, which has been chosen as representing a remedy often used to soothe physical suffering. And, as in sickness, the physician strives to apply his medicine to the root of the disease, so in Extreme Unction, the five senses, which are, so to speak, the chief instruments of sin, are anointed.

We must next consider the Sacrament of Holy Orders. As we do so, we shall see, with what good reason it has been ordained. When Christ withdrew His visible presence from the Church, it was necessary that He should have some representatives, who should dispense the Sacraments to the faithful. And, as they were to be His instruments, it was likewise necessary that they should be like, in some manner, to Himself, and thus be proportioned to their Agent. Christ, being both God and Man, His ministers had, then, to be, not angels, but men, endowed with some share of His Divine power. And, as they could not be immortal, they had to possess this power, in such a manner, as to be capable of conferring it on their successors, until the consummation of the world. This power, for reasons given above when treating of the Sacraments in general, has been fittingly bestowed upon the ministers of Christ, under the form of certain formulated words and signs, such as the imposition of hands, the presentation of the chalice and book, etc. But, as the power of Orders is given, to enable the ministers of the Church to administer the Sacraments — of which the Blessed Eucharist is the chief — we must consider the degrees of Orders, with relation to this adorable Sacrament.

We know that every power designed to produce an important effect, is served by other and inferior powers, even as an architect who intends to erect a building, is assisted by stonecutters, and other labourers. Since, then, the Sacrament of Holy Orders is instituted, mainly, in order to consecrate this Body and Blood of Christ, to distribute It to the faithful, and to cleanse them from sin — in order to prepare them for Its reception — there must be some rank or Order, destined, especially, for this office, and served by ministers of inferior degree. This rank is the Priesthood, which is created for two ends, viz., to consecrate the Body and Blood of Christ, and to cleanse the faithful, from sin, in order to enable them to receive It. Priests, then, must be assisted in both, or in one, of their offices, by those in lower orders, who will, according to their dignity, take part in rites more or less sacred. The lowest Order of door-keepers, is instituted in order to prepare the people, to separate the faithful from unbelievers, and to exclude the latter from the Church. Next in dignity comes the Order of Readers, whose duty it is to instruct neophytes in the Faith.

Then Exorcists, who must deliver them from the power of the devil. The office of those in the higher Orders is, to prepare the faithful for the Sacraments, and to assist in the celebration of the Blessed Eucharist. Thus the Acolyths must prepare the vessels and elements used in the Sacrifice; the Sub-deacons must place the uncon-secrated species in the sacred vessels; and the Deacons must also have some office with respect to the Consecrated Elements, inasmuch as they are ordained to distribute to the faithful the Precious Blood of Christ.

Hence, only Priests, Deacons, and Sub-deacons are said to be in Sacred Orders; this term signifying, that they alone, have power to handle that which is most Sacred. Deacons, Sub-deacons, and Acolyths also assist the priest in preparing the people. The Deacon reads the Gospel to them, and the Sub-deacon the Epistle, and the Acolyth bears the lights, which are intended to show reverence for the Holy Scripture.

And, as the Sacraments must be administered by fitting persons, appointed by some superior power, it is reasonable that Episcopal authority should exist in the Church, which, while nowise exceeding the sacerdotal power with regard to the Consecration of the Body of the Lord, is superior to the priestly power in all that pertains to the body of the Church, and the solution of any difficulties which may arise in its government. But, although there are many different bishops in many parts of the earth, — the Church being one, — the whole Christian people is under one head, and is thus united in one Faith, and in no danger of being divided by reason of different opinions springing up within the Church. The power given to the ministers of Christ is inalienable, and cannot be forfeited by any sin. And the Sacraments, administered by sinful priests, lose none, of their efficacy, since their virtue resides in the Sacraments themselves, not in their ministers. Neither do those who receive the Sacraments from unworthy priests, become themselves unworthy. For priests are only His instruments; and that on which an effect is wrought becomes like to the principal agent, not like to the instrument.

Finally, the Sacrament of Matrimony is a state most fittingly ordained, not only for the public welfare and for the preservation of the human, race, but likewise for the multiplication of the faithful, to the Glory of God. The union of man with woman, in so far as it concerns the good of the Church, is a true Sacrament, blessed by the ministers of Christ, representing the union of the Church with our Lord, and conferring grace on those that receive it devoutly. And as there is only one Christ and one Church; and as Matrimony represents the union between them; the bond of wedlock must be indissoluble, in order that God may be glorified and Holy Church perpetuated.

From what we have said, it is, we think, plain, that there is nothing unreasonable or impracticable in the principal ceremonies of the Church.

CHAPTER XVII.

ANSWERS TO CERTAIN OBJECTIONS BROUGHT AGAINST THE DOCTRINE OF THE BLESSED EUCHARIST.

Many and great difficulties are wont to arise in man's mind concerning the dogma of the Blessed Eucharist. We, therefore, deem it expedient, to devote some space to their consideration. When we declare that the whole Body of Christ is contained in a little bread, and His Blood in a little wine; and that, at the same time, the whole Christ is in Heaven; it seems as if we were affirming an impossibility. For Christ can only be present in this Sacrament in one of two ways. Either, the bread is changed into the Body of Christ; and this appears to be out of the question. For a thing into which another thing is changed, has no existence before this change; it only begins to exist when this change has taken place. If, then, the bread be changed into the Body of Christ, His Body cannot have existed before the bread was changed into It; just as the serpent into which the rod of Aaron was changed had no existence previous to this miracle. Thus, the Body of Christ which is in the Blessed Eucharist, is not the Body which is in Heaven, but another Body newly produced. Or else, we may say that the Body of Christ which is in Heaven, comes by local movement into the Blessed Sacrament. But this seems, likewise, impossible! Firstly, because, unless His Body left Heaven altogether, it would have to be in two places at once. Secondly, because local movement can- not terminate in more than one place at the same time; and we know that many Hosts are consecrated at once. Thirdly, because one Body cannot be in more than one place at the same moment. How, also, can a full-grown Body be contained in a little Host, and all Its Blood in a small chalice? Again, it seems impossible that accidents can exist without their substance; the more so as we know, by experience, that the consecrated bread and wine do what accidents alone could not do — (e.g., nourish, warm, and strengthen the body) — and that the consecrated wine, if consumed to excess, would produce intoxication.

Furthermore, the consecrated elements are subject to vicissitudes, such as burning, putrefaction, etc., which could not affect mere accidents. And, again, if the elements be divided into small particles, how can the Body of Christ be present in each fraction? Our answer to these objections is that we have made before ., viz., that the infinite power of God can do more than we can conceive; and that, what is impossible to nature and to man, is possible to Him. In the Blessed Eucharist there is nothing beyond the power of God. For we say that the Body and Blood of Christ are present in this Sacrament by conversion. And this is not impossible to God, although it is impossible to nature, which cannot change one thing into another thing already in existence.

If the infinite power of God can create something out of nothing, can it not, much more, cause one substance to be transformed into another, and therefore the substance of bread and wine to become the substance of the Body and Blood of Christ?

Since, then, the Body of Christ is not present in the Blessed Eucharist by local movement, i.e., by descent from Heaven into the Host, but solely by conversion, we must admit that His presence in Heaven differs modally from His sacramental presence. In Heaven His Body, like other bodies, occupies space and is extended; but He is present in the Host, not by mode of extension, but in an indivisible manner, and in a mode so wonderful, that this whole Body is present in every fragment of the Host. This mode of existence is possible only to God, whose power exceeds the bounds of our intelligence. But, observe, that in the Blessed Eucharist the Body of Christ is present under the appearance of bread, and His Blood under that of wine; but as His Blood, His Soul, and his Divinity never leave His Body, and His Body never leaves His Blood, the whole Christ is, by natural concomitance, present in every particle and drop of both species. Christ, further-more, is not present in this Sacrament as in a place.

Therefore, although there are many Hosts on many altars, He is not in many places but in many Sacraments. We see this in our own case, for we know that our whole soul is in every part of our body, and yet we do not say that it is in different places; because the soul is not in the body as in a place, but as the form in its matter.

As God has created all things out of nothing by His own Power, without the aid of other causes, He can pro-duce all natural effects without using secondary causes. Therefore, although, naturally speaking, substance up-holds accidents, God can preserve accidents without the help of substance. Many philosophers have maintained that quantity can exist without substance; and we say that in the Blessed Eucharist; not quantity only, but all other accidents, do, by the power of God, exist without substance. Not only does God enable accidents to exist without substance; but He enables them to do, and to suffer, that which substance would do and suffer, were the accidents joined to substance, e.g., to nourish, to intoxicate, to putrefy, to burn, etc. These actions and sufferings do not extend to the Body of Christ, but only to the accidents. Thus when the Host is broken, the fracture does not affect the Body of Christ, which remains entire in each particle. 21 Many other difficulties may be urged against the dogma of the Eucharist, but the solution we have given to the difficulties enumerated, will pave the way to the solution of all others. And it will be manifest that the Catholic Faith does not, in this doctrine, propose to our belief anything impossible to God.

CHAPTER XVIII.

THE REASONABLENESS OF THE CEREMONIES OF THE CHURCH.

Having shown that the Sacraments of the Church are in accordance with reason, it will not be difficult to prove that other ecclesiastical ceremonies are equally rational But as we Cannot, for the sake of brevity, discuss them all, we will confine our attention to a few of the most important.

First, then, the homage paid by Christians to the Cross, and to representations of Christ and of His Saints, may seem to some people irrational. We must, however, remember that images may be looked upon from two points of view. We may consider the material of which they are made, gold, silver, wood, or stone. Certainly, Christians do not honour images on this account. Or, we may consider images representing some Divine Person. And this is the light in which Christians regard them. They pay homage not to the image itself, but to the thing or person represented thereby; just as, when subjects honour a picture of their sovereign, they honor, not the picture itself, but him who is depicted thereon. Therefore we pay to images the honour due to those whom they represent. We give to the Cross and Crucifix the worship of latria, which is the worship that we pay to God. We honour an image of the Virgin Mary with an inferior honour, yet with greater honor than that which we give to representations of the other Saints. We honour the Saints as the blessed friends of God. We erect their images in order to recall them to our memory, to excite ourselves to virtue by their example, and to raise our hearts in prayer to God, through their intercession. There can be no doubt that pictures and statues, representing holy objects, are as helpful as books, especially to unlettered and simple folk.

And as we know invisible things by means of such as are visible, we build and consecrate material churches thereby symbolizing the spiritual Church, and enabling ourselves, by the sight of earthly things, to raise our minds to the contemplation of Divine mysteries. The stones of the church signify Christians united in Faith; and the lime which cements them is charity, which joins the hearts of the faithful together. The foundation-stone is Christ; and the stones around it represent the Prophets and Apostles. The high walls symbolize the sublimity of the contemplative life; the roof the active life, exposed to the storms of temptation. The spiritual temple differs from an earthly edifice in that its foundation is in Heaven.

In the length of the church, we behold the permanence of the true Church; in its height, the difference of merit among its members; and in its breadth, the number of the faithful throughout the world. The sanctuary recalls to us the Virgins of Christ, and the naves those living in the married state; for as the sanctuary is narrower and more holy than the naves, virginity is holier and rarer than wedlock. The cemetery in front of the church reminds us of false Christians buried in sin. The altar represents Christ, on whom we offer our sacrifices, saying at the end of every prayer, "Through our Lord Jesus Christ". The belfry signifies the Holy Scripture, by means of which, (if we take our stand upon it), we shall be able to discern the snares of our enemies, and to fight against them. The bells are preachers calling together the Church militant and triumphant. The windows we may take to represent the holy doctors who pour the light of their teaching into the Church. From the whiteness of the interior walls we learn purity of heart and external decorum. The twelve candles, burning before the crosses of consecration, represent the twelve Apostles, who have enlightened the world by preaching the Cross of Christ throughout it. The doors signify the Sacraments, by means of which, especially of Baptism, we enter the Church. The lamps symbolize the continual illumination of the Holy Ghost The Holy Water may remind us of the tears of penitents. Finally the sacred vestments and vessels, the psalms, hymns, and the whole order of ceremonies, represent the Divine mysteries, which time will not permit us to explain. But from what has been said, it is evident, that nothing contained in Christian doctrine is either incredible or unreasonable.

If anyone desires further instruction, and will read, and carefully reflect on, the works of the Doctors of the Church, he will understand that our religion is the work, not of men, but, of Him "who enlightens every man that Comes into this world". Daily experience proves to us, that many good men, reflecting upon these mysterious rites, forget themselves, are raised above worldly thoughts and earthly things, and that their "conversation is in heaven".

BOOK IV.

INTRODUCTION.

METHOD OBSERVED THROUGHOUT THIS BOOK.

Would that all men were sincerely zealous in the pursuit of truth. It would then be far easier to open their eyes to perceive it, for their intellect tending towards it, as to its perfection, would readily incline to embrace it. Indeed some men are so strongly attracted to truth, that they utter it even against their will.

The knowledge of a thing leads to the knowledge of its opposite; for instance, if we know the right side we shall know the left; and if we know what is true, we shall easily know what is false. And, although truth is at constant war with falsehood, nevertheless, he that draws nigh to truth, will ever be victorious. Therefore, when different and contrary opinions prevail among men, that opinion may be held to be most probably true which is supported by the soundest reasoning. Now, as there exists much discord amongst men on matters of religion, and the arguments in favour of Christianity are much stronger than those that can be advanced in support of any other form...of belief, Christianity must indubitably be the true religion. This is the point which we shall undertake in this Book to prove, first in general, and then in particular.

CHAPTER I.

NO RELIGION EXCEPT CHRISTIANITY CAN BE TRUE.

From what has just been said, it is evident, that Christianity is the only true religion. And if this be the case, and if there be no salvation except through the faith of Christ, all, save Christians, must be living in error.

Again, if a virtuous life be the end proposed by all religions, and if there be no better life than the Christian life, there can be no religion superior to Christianity. Any other religion must be either equal or inferior to it. If other religions be inferior to Christianity, Christianity must be the best; and we are bound to embrace it, and to reject all others as idle and superstitious. But if there be a religion equal to Christianity, it must be the same as Christianity. For, unless it propose to us the same end to be attained, and the same means for the attainment of that end, as Christianity professes, it cannot be called equal; it must be inferior to the Christian creed.

Furthermore, if we know a cause by its effects, and if Christian holiness be the perfection of human life; and, if we see no such effects produced by any other religion, Christianity must be true; the more so, as its effects are so quickly and so easily produced, and as its power appears so marvelously in the conversion of men.

Therefore, there can be no danger of erring in rejecting all other creeds, and cleaving to the faith of Christ.

In order, however, to make what we say more clear, we will descend to particulars, and will discuss divers forms of religion. But, as it would be useless to attempt to discuss all the superstitions which have ever existed, we will reduce them to six; viz. heathen philosophy, astrology, idolatry, Judaism, heresy, and Mahometanism.

In our analysis of these false religions, we will ignore the different opinions and divisions which have existed amongst philosophers, astrologers, idolaters, and heretics. We will examine their tenets from a general point of view.

CHAPTER II.

THE DEFECTIVE AND ERRONEOUS RELIGIONS TAUGHT BY HEATHEN PHILOSOPHERS.

We must preface our remarks by observing that the teaching of heathen philosophy, even where its leaders have not taught erroneous doctrine, is, in all that regards salvation, exceedingly poor and insufficient. Nor can we wonder at this, seeing that their only guide was the light of human reason. For, as the end to which we aspire must be the rule of all our operations, those who undertake to lead men to a virtuous way of living ought, at least, to know what is the true end of human life. Now, the heathen sages could have no such knowledge, because it exceeds the bounds of human reason, by which alone they were enlightened. But if they could not know the last end of man, still less could they know by what means he could attain his end. Therefore, all that they could teach about religion was necessarily imperfect, uncertain, or erroneous. What sane person, then, would abandon Christianity, for the tenets of heathen philosophy?

And, although, the best among the philosophers held that the end of human life is the contemplation of Divine things, their teaching on this point is very confused, because they cannot speak, with any certainty, about their end. If they were asked, whether, by this contemplation, they meant contemplation of this present life, or of the future life, they could not answer with any certainty. For, considering the perils and troubles of this life, it would be wholly unreasonable to expect beatitude in it; and as the philosophers could not, by means of mere natural reason, discover anything about the future life, whatever they might say about it would be unproven, and therefore not accepted by men. They would, furthermore, involve themselves in the still more intricate question of the immortality of the soul, the difficulty of which is shown by the many different opinions entertained concerning it. The greatest difficulty on this point arises from the fact, that, as the soul can perform the operation of understanding without any corporeal organ, it would appear, that, with regard to the activity of understanding, the soul cannot be the form of the body; for it seems as if that which can act without a body, can exist without a body. This is why Plato insisted that our soul is not: the form, but the mover of the human body.

Aristotle, on the contrary , maintains that the soul is the form of the body. He, however, uses such ambiguous expressions about the understanding, as distinct from the soul, that his commentator, Averroes, fell into the unreasonable error of supposing that there is in all men an intellect, existing independently of other powers. But, I believe that Aristotle, being a very sagacious man and knowing that the natural light of reason cannot arrive at any perfect knowledge of the matter, purposely spoke very cautiously about it, for fear of being worsted in argument. Thus the philosophers who followed him, remained in a dilemma. For, if they called the soul the form of the body, it seemed that the soul must reasonably be supposed to be mortal. If they said that the soul was not the form of the body, it was impossible to see how man could be said to be man, on account of his possessing an intellectual soul. And, if, with no clearer light than the light of natural reason, they had maintained what Faith teaches, viz., that although the intellectual power of the soul operates independently of any corporeal organ, yet, nevertheless, the substance of the soul is the form of the body, they would have found themselves in quite as great a difficulty as they were before. For they would have been asked, whence came this form — a question to which they could have given no certain answer. For, as this form is elevated above all corporeal things, it cannot have been produced by any natural power; nor, as they did not believe in creation, would these philosophers have said that it came from nothing. And, even if they had made such an assertion, they could not have produced any reasonable proof of what they said. Their opinion, consequently, would have been treated with contempt.

Certain ones amongst them, therefore, endeavoured to evade the difficulty, by maintaining that souls existed from eternity, before bodies. This opinion, however, involved them in still greater confusion. For, while they held that souls were made from eternity before bodies, they could adduce no reason to hinder the soul from being the form of the body. They, also, at the same time, fell into many other inconsistencies, adduced by the Peripatetics against the Platonists. And, although Aristotle said that the intellectual soul comes from without, i.e., not from natural power, — his expression is very ambiguous; for it ex plains neither whence, nor how, the soul comes into the world. And if, as he maintains, the intellectual soul be immortal, and the form of the body, it cannot, at the same time, exist before the body, nor pass from one body to another. Therefore, if the soul be not produced by natural power, I do not see how Aristotle can deny Creation.

The philosophers who, unenlightened by faith, assert that the soul is immortal, and is the form of the body, expose themselves to further difficulties. They may,

with good reason, be asked whether the world has likewise existed from eternity, and whether it will last forever. If they reply, without being able to prove their words, that the world had a beginning and will have an end, their views will be held in derision. If, on the other
hand, with Aristotle, they maintain that the world never had a beginning and will never have an end, they must likewise hold that there has existed an infinite series of years and days. But, if man is the most important part of the world, no one can, with any show of reason, say that the world has existed without man; and therefore infinite men must have died. If, further, as they say, the soul is immortal, and is the form of the body; and if it does not pass from one body to another, there must have been infinite souls. This is, clearly, an irrational hypothesis. Those who uphold this view will, of course, maintain that it is not irrational; but by so doing, they have to face fresh difficulties. For, as the soul is the form of the body, it is against its nature to be outside the body; and we know, in fact, that the soul only leaves the body by compulsion. Now, compulsion, or violence, cannot continue perpetually, especially in the case of so noble a thing as the soul.

Those, however, who hold that souls will never return to their bodies, must admit that souls, in spite of their dignity, are perpetually banished, by violence, from their bodies. If they believe in the resurrection of the body, on the other hand, they must believe in the resurrection of infinite bodies, which is impossible. They may, indeed, hold, that, after a certain prolonged space of time, souls will return to their former bodies, and will become what they formerly were; and that they will repeat this separation from, and return to, their bodies an infinite number of times. But they have no reason, or proof, on which to ground this hypothesis; and we are right in treating it with contempt. And, certainly, such a supposition is unreasonable and absurd, implying, as it does, that we, and all that exist at present, must have already existed an infinite number of times.

In these, and in such like difficulties, do they entangle themselves who try, by natural reason, to discover the end of human life. Nor, as they ignore the most important element of life, can they be expected to speak surely or definitely, either about religion or about virtuous living. We need not, therefore, be surprised, that the religious systems of the philosophers are imperfect, and filled with error.

We shall understand this fact still more clearly, if we consider the different erroneous conclusions at which they have arrived; and we shall see how poor and feeble a thing is the unassisted light of reason. The highest power of an agent is shown when it exerts itself to its fullest capacity. Now, human reason has been most strenuously exerted by the greatest philosophers, who have exercised it to the utmost of their ability. We see this by the fact, that the other philosophers who have succeeded them, have never found anything new to say; or if they have originated some fresh theory, it has been a very insignificant one. Since, then, the very greatest philosophers have been so grossly mistaken in matters concerning salvation, it is evident that the natural light of reason is but a treacherous guide.

Of course, the earliest philosophers, who asserted that the last end of man is to be found in riches, glory, pleasure, or some other material good, were far more completely deceived than those who taught that it was

193

to be sought in the contemplation of Divine things. But, the teaching of these latter was vague, and left men in the greatest uncertainty about the affairs of their salvation.

Again, there are as many opinions and errors about the nature of the intellectual soul, as there are philosophers. Setting aside the fallacies enumerated by Aristotle in his first book, De Anima, even the Aristotelian philosophers themselves entertain endless different views. Some teach that the human understanding is one thing, and others proclaim it to be another; so that, even to this day, their disciples remain in utter uncertainty. This confusion would be even more inextricable, had not the Faith of Christ enlightened the world.

Again, if any one will read the philosophical books treating of the universe, of the end for which it was made, and of its supposed beginning and end, he will find almost as many errors as there are words. And, although Aristotle, and some of his followers, have tried to establish the eternity of the world, the Aristotelian arguments are so weak, that any learned man could easily overthrow them.

But what are we to say of the number of the angels, or, as the philosophers call them, the separate substances? Aristotle, following the motion of the heavens, represents the angels as being equal in number to the celestial spheres, as though they were created solely to move the heavens. This is, of course, an absurdity. It is probable, however, that Aristotle spoke, not as affirming a certainty, but as giving an opinion.

Again, the heathen schools of philosophy, besides

their many grave errors, laid down nothing definite or certain about the externals of Divine worship. They entertained also any most frivolous ideas about Divine Providence. And thus, their teaching, far from being profitable to man's salvation, or honourable to religion, was merely a source of confusion to mankind. Nevertheless, we must not despise the valuable portion of the old philosophy, but rather make use of it ourselves. For, although it is not sufficient for salvation, it is often of great assistance to us in confuting the adversaries of the Faith.

CHAPTER III.

THE FUTILITY AND SUPERSTITION OF THE TRADITIONS OF ASTROLOGY.

ASTROLOGERS, who claim to be reputed philosophers, maintain that human affairs are governed by the heavens and the stars, making out the sky to be our god, thus imitating some of the ancients, who worshipped the sun and the stars. We will, therefore, with the plainest arguments, demonstrate their error, and show that the heavenly bodies are not the cause of the things which man performs by means of his understanding and his will. Superior things cannot be governed by their inferiors; hence, as the intellect is more perfect than any mere body, it cannot be governed by either heavenly or any other bodies.

Again, it has been proved by philosophers, that no body operates without movement. Consequently, im-movable things, such as incorporeal substances, amongst which is the intellect, are not subject to bodies. Hence we see that the understanding, in proportion to its abstraction from the restlessness and activity of things corporeal, works with greater rapidity and greater perfection.

We know, likewise, that everything that is ruled or moved, whether by heavenly or earthly bodies, is physical, and subject to time. Now, our understanding transcends, in its operations, all bodies, and extends to immaterial things, and even to God. This it could not do by means of any physical force; for, no agent, in its operations, exceeds its nature. Hence, the power of the heavenly bodies cannot, strictly speaking, act upon our understanding, since the power of the understanding far surpasses that of the firmament.

Many believers in astrology, being hard pressed by this argument, try to evade the difficulty by saying, that the heavenly bodies are not the direct, but the indirect cause of the operations of our understanding. The intellect (they argue) makes use of sensitive powers, especially of imagination, memory, and thought, which are dependent on physical temperament; and, as our body, like all other composite bodies, is subject to the heavenly bodies, these heavenly bodies do, in a certain sense, influence our understanding. We all know, of course, that difference of mental endowment is the result of difference of temperament. But no one who reflects on the nature of the understanding or of free-will, can possibly believe, that the heavens can in any way influence our choice, or rule the course of human events. Everything that happens from the impression of the celestial bodies, happens naturally; being naturally subject to these bodies. Hence, if the operations of free-will were the result of the impression of these bodies, these operations would be natural and not voluntary, originating not from free-will, but from natural animal instinct. The absurdity of this opinion can be easily demonstrated.

First, we know that all things which act by natural instinct, proceed", if they be of the same nature, to the same end, by the same means, and in the same manner; just as all heavy things tend to their centre. But men, both in natural and artificial things, tend to different ends, using different means. Therefore, their operations are not natural, but voluntary. Secondly, natural operations are always, or almost always, well ordered; for nature very seldom errs; whereas human operations are not always free from error. Thirdly, natural operations, in so far as they are natural, do not vary; — thus, all swallows build their nests and feed their young in the same way; and sparrows, and every species of bird, follow their own specific method of carrying on these operations. But, human operation's are so diverse, that we see scarcely two men who act alike; the reason being that man is guided, not by instinct, but by free will. Again, did human choice depend on nature, virtue and vice must be imputed not to individuals but to nature; which view would destroy all idea of injustice, or of rational plan, or of a providence over human affairs. Since nature is governed by God and is immutable, man would necessarily be left to act according to his instinct. We can imagine what would then be the condition of human affairs.

But, to return to our first proposition. Since the understanding exceeds, in its operations, all bodies, the will exceeds them likewise; because its love and desire aspire even to God. Therefore, the will cannot be subject to any physical power. Further, as means are proportioned to their end; and as the last end of man exceeds any corporeal thing; the operations of the understanding and of the will, by means of which man attains his end, transcend all bodies; nor are they subject to the influence of the heavenly bodies. And, although our bodies are subject to celestial bodies, and are, by the impressions made on us by them, inclined to do what is contrary to right reason; we have, nevertheless, so much power to resist this inclination, that our operations may be said to be subject, not to the heavens, but to our free-will. Thus, as the firmament is not, strictly speaking, the cause of our actions, it cannot be called our God. For God is the First Cause, who does all things, and acts in all things.

Some however, maintain that the heavenly bodies are animate. They, therefore, hold that, although of themselves they do not move our understanding and free-will, these faculties are, nevertheless, influenced by the soul which vivifies the heavens. The following arguments will easily demonstrate the fallacy of this opinion : —

First, it is futile to use an instrument which is not adapted to produce a desired effect. It has already been proved that the power of the heavens is not able to influence the understanding and free will. It is futile, therefore, to say that the heavenly bodies, as instruments of the soul which animates the firmament, act upon our understanding.

Secondly, the soul of the heavens cannot of by means of its instruments, the celestial bodies, affect immediately or directly, the intellect or will, because corporeal influences cannot immediately act upon what is spiritual. But the power of the heavenly bodies may, certainly, affect our physical temperament, and by means of it may influence our imagination and interior sense. These activities, in their turn, may represent to our understanding some advantage to be sought, or peril to be avoided. But no one is obliged to heed these phantasies. We are always free to think, or not to think of what we choose; and experience proves that man is master of his actions. Therefore, it is unreasonable to say that the stars and the firmament, or the soul which animates them, is God. For God is He who immediately gives being and operation to all things; it is He who moves our understanding and free-will; although in moving it He always respects our liberty, because He moves all things in a way that is adapted to their nature. Therefore, all worship given to the heavens, or to the stars, or to the soul of the firmament, is empty and dangerous. These bodies are created for the service of man; and no one ought to worship that which is meant to be his servant. Hence, we see the folly of astrologers who assign to the heavens the government of human affairs, and pretend to direct men by observation of the stars.

But, even in these modern times, there are some nominal Christians, who, under certain disguises, try to uphold the fallacies of astrology. They say, for instance, that although free-will is, by its nature, subject, not to the heavens, but to God; nevertheless, since the sensitive part of our nature — by which almost all men are ruled — is subject to astral influences, they are able by means of the stars to foretell many future events; the more so, that God governs human affairs by means of the stars, as secondary causes. So far, indeed, does the father of lies lead them astray, that they delude men into trusting more to the stars than to God, and they are able to persuade them to undertake nothing without first consulting the heavens.

This system of astrological divination so little deserves the name of science, or of art, that the Best philosophers have judged it unworthy of notice, and have passed it over in silence. Both Plato and Aristotle ignore it. The latter proves, in many places, that we can have no knowledge of the things to which astrology professes to furnish a clue. For, future events, which may or may not take place, cannot be known in themselves, as they as yet possess no being; nor can they be foreseen in their cause, since they have no definite or determinate cause, but only such as is uncertain and wholly undetermined.

But, granted that man could arrive at some knowledge of the future, he certainly could not attain to it by looking at the heavens, as the universal cause of inferior things. Certainly no knowledge of particular effects can be attained by the contemplation of a general cause, but only by the investigation of proximate and particular causes. Physicians do not try to discover the causes of sickness by means of the stars, nor do they endeavour to cure by an astrolabe; they study, rather, to find out the special predisposing causes of illness, and the physical temperament of their patient. Nothing, therefore, can be more foolish than to attempt to investigate, by the mere contemplation of the stars and planets, future events, which will arise from the free-will of individuals and from particular causes.

Astrologers say that different virtues and properties reside in different parts of the heavens. The absurdity of this pretension shows the folly of their other superstitions. The very greatest philosophers, who, certainly, were far wiser and better informed than astrologers, have never discovered in the firmament, the virtue claimed for it by astrologers. The astrologers further affirm that this virtue or property acts upon the earth by means of the moon and of the motion of the firmament, and that the variety of things caused upon earth proceeds, primarily, from the diversity of light and from the motions of the spheres and of the stars; and, secondarily, from the variety of the dispositions of matter and of particular agents. Hence, according to their opinion, if we wish to foretell future events, it does not suffice to know the varieties of light and of motion in the heavens; we must also understand the disposition of matter, and the nature of particular agents, without which the celestial bodies cannot act. But, since, for reasons before stated, we could not, even if we had this knowledge, arrive at any certainty as to the future — especially as to events which depend on free-will — how can we be likely to gain such certainty, merely by gazing at the stars?

But, even if we assume with astrologers, that Divine properties reside in the heavens, this does not prove that their astrology is not foolish. For such properties can be nothing but the universal causes of the things which take place on earth. For, as the stars and planets are more remote from earth than are the elements, and as the elements are universal causes of terrestrial things, the celestial bodies must be causes even more universal. Now, we cannot, merely by understanding the generative force of animated beings in general, know the mode of reproduction peculiar to particular species of animated life — such as animals or plants. Still less can we arrive at such knowledge merely by contemplating the heavens.

But although it is an absurdity, let us concede to astrologers, that the virtue of the astral' bodies is more particular than that of the elements. Their divination would still remain an idle folly; for our senses, (which are the fount of our knowledge), can never investigate anything so far remote from them as the forces of the heavens. The greatest philosophers have never discovered these forces. We cannot understand the properties even of many things which we handle every day; and how can astrologers, who cannot compare either in mental capacity or in learning with philosophers, pretend to analyze the powers of the stars? But, even if they did understand these powers, they would have no reason to boast of their idle superstitions. For the particular causes, existing under heaven, cannot have been created in vain, since nothing has been made without a purpose.

If, then, there reside in the firmament certain particular forces, e.g. one destined to reproduce mankind, another to reproduce oxen, etc., we should have to say, that sublunary particular causes exist, only for the purpose of disposing matter for the reception of the form impressed on them by astral forces. Therefore, for the purposes of divination, an astrologer could not be satisfied by the mere contemplation of the heavens. The heavenly bodies impress different forms upon matter, according to its varying disposition; and if matter be not duly prepared, it is incapable of receiving a form. And, as there may be many obstacles to the fitting preparation of matter, an astrologer could not gain any sure knowledge of particular things by merely gazing at the skies. For instance, let us suppose that the force contained in one particular star is adapted to produce grapes from a vine. We cannot, by merely gazing at the star, calculate the crop which that vine will bear; for, many things may
hinder its fertility. It may be, for example, planted in unsuitable soil; it may be cut down; cattle may browse on it; or some other star may injure it, by causing either drought or too heavy rains. By merely looking at the sky we cannot know which of these, and many similar accidents, may occur. And if we can arrive at no more certain conclusion than this, about purely natural things, how much less can we trust our judgment upon those points which depend on the endless variations of free will?

Therefore, when we consider the false principles on which astrology is based, and the mutable nature of man's desires and will, we shall see very clearly that the conduct of human affairs does not depend on the stars, and that it is an absurdity to try to direct man's lives by studying the heavens.

But, it is not our intention to argue at any greater length against such folly. We will rest content with having proved that any religion, that ever has been, or ever shall be invented, for the worship of the stars and other heavenly bodies, is meaningless and superstitious. Count Giovanni Pico della Mirandola, whose sublimity of intelligence and wealth of learning must be numbered among the great works of God and of nature, has, in his book of disputations, so subtly confuted and completely demolished the pretensions of astrologers to powers of divination, that anyone who reads his treatise intelligently, and does not then despise astrology, deserves to be considered an unreasonable man. In order, furthermore, to convince everyone of the folly of astrologers, I also have composed and published, in the vulgar tongue, 22 a work in confutation of their doctrine. Therefore, let whosoever desires it read these books, and he will see how great a folly it is to devote time to such a superstition, or to trust in it.

CHAPTER IV.

IDOLATRY IS OF ALL THINGS THE MOST VAIN.

We have already shown that the religion of philosophers, who worshipped the First Cause, was insufficient for salvation; and that the teaching of astrologers was most useless and dangerous. How much more contemptible, then, is worship given to images of wood and stones made in the likeness of men or beasts? Surely, such a religion needs no confutation; since everyone can see that it is foolish to honour senseless things.

Some men, however, to excuse their folly, say that they do not honour images themselves, but the gods dwelling in them, just as Christians honour the representations of the Saints. We shall show, therefore, that the worship which they pay to these gods, was, and if it still anywhere exist, is, both impious and superstitious. This is a fitting place to discuss this subject; for, as we have been treating of extremes we ought now to speak of the mean; and midway between God and the heavens, are the separate substances 23 which were the gods of the pagans.

But we must remember that God moves the will of man in two ways : either by showing him good, in order to excite him to the love of it; or, by applying His power to the will of man, in order to make that will elicit an act of love or of desire — just as a shepherd may either attract a sheep by showing it pasturage; or he may, with his hand, draw it along. Now, creatures can influence each other in the former of these two ways; but no man can act on the will of another in the second way specified. Because, as the will proceeds immediately from God, it

is immediately subject lo Him, and Re alone can move it to will, or not to will. But, although the will be completely in God's power. He never acts upon it in such a way as to deprive man of his liberty. He always leaves him his free will; because God moves all things according to their form and natural propensity. Man, as man, is immediately subject to God; and to Him alone, as to the Prime Mover and Ruler of all things, does he owe the worship of latria. 24 He is bound to pay to other immaterial substances, only such honour as is proportioned to their participation in the Divine likeness. Therefore, the Christian gives all his worship to God. He honours the Saints and Angels, not as gods but as the friends of God. He desires that they should pray for him, and impetrate from God the things that he, of himself, cannot obtain from Him. He praises God in His Saints, and thanks Him that He has deigned to bestow such glory upon His creatures. This is a lawful and holy way of honouring God and immaterial substances. But
idolaters adored their idols, and burnt incense to them, and implored favours of them, believing them to be true gods.

But, as some may argue that, although the heathens adored many gods, their worship was really referred to Almighty God, whom they adored in all their other gods; we shall show that, even were this the case, it would notjustify the folly and evil of idolatry. Firstly, because the masses of the heathen nations could not appreciate such distinctions, and were, therefore, misled; and, secondly, because the heathen ceremonies were largely composed of absurd and unseemly rites. It cannot be maintained that these ceremonies were practiced only by impious men who wanted to degrade the worship of their idols, since they were observed throughout the whole world, even amongst great men.

But we will not now argue this point any further.
We will confine ourselves to proving, that the idols,
worshipped by the heathen, were not gods, but evil spirits
in whose person God could not be honoured. It is
proper to every created and well-ordered intellect, not
only to submit itself, and to pay homage to its First
Cause, which is God; but also to dispose all other intel-
ligences inferior to itself, to do likewise, so that God, the
Worker of all good, may be glorified in all things. But
the spirits adored by idolaters, whilst frequently giving
answers to those who questioned them, never inclined men
to true religion, nor to a well-ordered life. In fact, we read
that they acted quite contrariwise, subverting all order,
deceiving men, and usurping the honour due to God; thus
filling the world with so much sin and
ignorance, that mankind had no knowledge of Him.

Again, good spirits do not work evil, nor encourage
hatred, nor inculcate vice. But we read of the pagan
deities, that amongst them, war, dissensions, sacrilege,
incest, and many other crimes, which we cannot contemplate without horror, were common; and these fabulous
stories of their lives set a bad example to all mankind.

Furthermore, God being perfect and standing in need
of nothing, does not, for His own sake, desire our worship.

He enjoins it on us for our profit, as a means whereby
we may become perfect and blessed. Therefore, every
well-ordered intelligence ought to endeavour, as far as
possible, to obey this Divine command, and to teach
others to worship God, in order thus to gain beatitude.
Consequently, had the heathen deities been good spirits,

they would have endeavoured to render men virtuous and perfect in the spiritual life, which consists in the knowledge, love, and desire of God. Now, on the contrary, they deceived mankind by so much vanity and falsehood, that, truth and virtue were far better taught in the schools of such philosophers as Pythagoras and Socrates, Plato and Aristotle, than in the temples of the gods. And the philosophers, who despised or ignored the pagan religions, were men of better life than the heathen priests.

Further, if the heathen deities had been good spirits, they would have given to mankind some assurance of obtaining what it desired, to wit, beatitude and true virtue; thereby showing that they watched over the interests of man as guardians, whose duty it was to direct all things to their proper end; and remembering that, even philosophers could not, by reason of this weakness of human intellect, arrive at knowledge of this truth. But, far from acting thus, the pagan gods confused the minds of mortals, and prevented them from attaining to this knowledge.

Good spirits are not liars, and do not deceive men; for falsehood is always evil. But we read of the gods of the ancients, that they frequently misled their questioners by giving them false and ambiguous answers. Again, as we have shown before, the knowledge of things to come is a Divine prerogative, which, had the heathen gods been good spirits, they would not have claimed. For they did not, like our prophets, say, "Thus says God". They spoke as of themselves, pretending to prescience of the future, and seducing men in to superstition. They also feigned to disclose to them events to come by means of the entrails of animals, or the song and flight of birds, and such like follies. From all this, good spirits would not only have abstained; they would even have forbidden them to their followers. Neither would good spirits have encouraged magical arts, by means of which, gross immorality was often perpetrated, innocent persons were deprived of life, and wicked men were rendered prosperous. On the contrary, they would have loathed such practices, and would have strenuously forbidden them.

Again, no good spirit would take pleasure in cruelty. Now, we read that, for the sacrifices offered to the heathen deities, not only were beasts slaughtered, but even children and young maidens were slain by their own fathers; and this, because the gods desired these massacres, and delighted in them. And, at the destruction of the pagan temples, which ensued on the preaching of the Apostles, there were found innumerable bones of men and women, but mostly of children, of both sexes.

We could recount endless evils which have sprung from idolatry. What we have said will, however, suffice, seeing that, through the mercy of our Lord Jesus Christ, this false teaching has been swept from the face of the earth. The heathen religions have likewise been abundantly confuted and expounded by our forefathers, who were men of learning. Surely if the pagan idols had been gods, their worship could never have been so completely exterminated as it has been.

CHAPTER V.

A REFUTATION OF THE JEWISH PERFIDY AND SUPERSTITION.

From what we have been saying it is clear, that, before the coming of Christ, the light of natural reason was obscured to such a degree, that, without His succour, mankind would have been so blinded by sin as to sink below the level of irrational animals. Therefore, man required supernatural light. But, as many, (among whom the Jews are the chief), have made a bad use of the knowledge which is the origin of this light, we intend to dispute with them, and to show them their errors; although they glory in the Old Testament, which they pervert by strained and erroneous interpretations. Now, all their hope is centered on the Messiah, for whose coming they still look. If, then, we are able to prove to them that the Messiah has already come, and is Jesus

Christ our Saviour, they cannot deny that our religion is of God, and that they are in error. And, although the proofs given in our Second Book ought to be sufficient to convince them, (for if Jesus be not the Messiah, who, greater or worthier than He, can come?), we will, nevertheless, adduce some further special arguments founded on those very Scriptures in which the Jews believe. We shall, however, discuss these points very briefly, as they have already been very fully treated by learned men.

We have promised in this Book to make use, not of the testimony of authority, but of reasoning. Our reasoning, as it is based on the authority in which our adversaries believe, is most convincing against them, and most profitable to other unbelievers. Therefore, on the author ity of the Prophets, we shall prove that Jesus Christ of Nazareth , crucified by the Jews, is the Messiah of the

Patriarchs and Prophets, and that He was, in many ways, foretold and foreshadowed in Holy Writ.

First, however, we must establish some self-evident principles. It was known to all the Jews, that God had promised to send them a Saviour and a great Prophet, who should be called the Messiah, and whom all men were to hear and obey as God Himself Thus Moses says to the people :"The Lord thy God will raise up to thee a Prophet of thy nation and of thy brethren like unto me : Him thou shalt hear, as thou desires of the Lord thy God"(Deut. 18:15, 16). And, again, the Lord speaks in these terms to Moses :"I will raise them up a Prophet out of the midst of their brethren, like to thee : and I will put My words in his mouth, and he shall speak to them all that I shall command him. And he that will not hear his words, which he shall speak in My name, I will be the revenger"(Ibid. 18:19,).

It is certain, then, and acknowledged by all the Jews, that the circumstances of the Messiah were foretold in the Mosaic law, in the Psalms, and in the Prophets. That is to say, there are many predictions concerning His race, birthplace, and the time of His coming, and also regarding His life and teaching. His works, and many other things peculiar to the Messiah. It is known, moreover, throughout the entire world, that the Old Testament, interpreted by Christian doctors, shows that all that is written of the Messiah is true of Jesus of Nazareth . In fact, so aptly do the prophecies of the Old Testament apply to Christ and to His Church, that if the Jews were not loud in proclaiming the antiquity of Moses and the Prophets, their predictions might be taken for forgeries of Christianity.

Let us, then, inquire of the Jews, whether Jesus of Nazareth be, in truth, the Messiah. If He be, they ought to become Christians; for they have been commanded to hear and to obey Him. If He be not the Messiah, how is it that God has allowed all the conditions peculiar to the Messiah to be manifested to the Jews, since He enjoined of them to follow Him who should display these qualifications? If Christ be not the Messiah, we must say, either that God did not know that Jesus was to come into the world, or that he could not prevent His coming; or that, having the power. He had not the will, to oppose His advent. Any of these answers would be unworthy of a sane man. If, then, God foreknew the coming of Christ, and could have prevented it, why did He not do so, since he had imposed such strict commandments upon the Jews? It would look as if God had deceived the Jews; and as if Christians would not be condemned by Him for following Jesus of Nazareth, in describing whose career all the Prophets agree, and who was wonderful above all other men. Certainly, if He be not the Messiah, we need not expect any greater wonder-worker than He. If He be not the Messiah, God, through Him, has deceived the whole human race. Let the Jews, then, search the Scripture, and see what distinguishing mark they expect to see in their Messiah, which is not clearly manifested by Jesus of Nazareth.

Again, Holy Writ foretells the period in which the Messiah is to come. This period, as we perceive by the Scripture, is long since passed. If, then, no man has ever been seen on earth, possessing greater power, wisdom, or goodness than Jesus of Nazareth, how can we doubt, that, if the Messiah be already come, Jesus was He? Many passages in Holy Scripture indicate the

time fixed for the advent of the Messiah. Thus we read in Genesis :"The scepter shall not be taken away from Juda, nor a ruler from his thigh, till He come that is to be sent, and He shall be the expectation of nations" (Gen. 49:10). Again in Daniel we read:"Seventy weeks are shortened upon thy people, and upon thy holy city, that transgression may be finished, and sin may have an end, and iniquity may be abolished; and everlasting justice may be brought; and vision and prophecy may be fulfilled; and the Saint of saints may be anointed. Know thou, therefore, and take notice: that from the going forth of the word, to build up Jerusalem again, unto Christ the prince, there shall be seven weeks, and sixty-two weeks : and the street shall be built again, and the walls in straitness of times. And after sixty-two weeks Christ shall be slain: and the people that deny Him shall not be His. And a people, with their leader that shall come, shall destroy the city and the sanctuary : and the end thereof shall be waste, and after the end of the war the appointed desolation. And he shall confirm the covenant with many, in one week: and in the half of the week the victim and the sacrifice shall fail: and there shall be in the temple the abomination of desolation: and the desolation shall continue even to the
consummation, and to the end" (Dan. 9:24-27).

We can easily see from these words, that Jesus Christ is the true Messiah. For the seventy weeks mentioned have passed long' ago; and there is no one except Christ with whom we can connect them. In the Holy Scriptures, as we learn from Leviticus 23 and 25., a week may signify either seven days or seven years. Now, seventy weeks of years amount to 490 years. And this period has elapsed, four times, between the days of Daniel and our own. And, if any one should object, that Daniel meant by a week neither seven days nor seven years, but some longer period, we would ask him what the longer period may be? And as he will not be able to answer, except in our terms, it is clear that any period assigned by him, and unspecified by Holy Writ, will be his own invention. Surely, if by a week God intended to signify a number of days and years not mentioned in Scripture, He would, by not apprising Daniel of the fact, have rendered his prophecy useless, and a cause of confusion and error. It must, therefore, be conceded that the time appointed for the advent of the Messiah is past; and, 'that He has already come. It were vain to answer, that, although the weeks predicted by Daniel have elapsed, the Messiah has not arrived; and to argue that neither Daniel nor the other Prophets indicate how soon after the close of the seventy weeks Christ is to come. For, if this argument held good, it would follow that the Prophets never foretold, with any certainty, anything concerning the Messiah. However, Daniel expressly says, "Know thou, therefore, and take notice : that from the going forth of the word, to build up Jerusalem again, unto Christ the Prince, there shall be seven weeks, and sixty-two weeks"; and again :"He shall confirm the covenant with many, in one week: and in the half of the week the victim and the sacrifice shall fail". The meaning of which words cannot certainly be applied to anyone except to Christ. Thus we see that He is indicated by this text; otherwise God would have led US into error, letting us believe that what was spoken concerning another, referred to Christ.

But let us now proceed to an exposition of the words. It is manifest, from what has already been said, that Jesus came into the world, in order to dispel error, and to lead men to holiness of life. Hence, the time of His coming is plainly shown by the words, "seventy weeks are shortened upon thy people, and upon thy holy city"; for they indicate that He was to preach first to the Jews. And the next words, "that transgression may be finished, and sin may have an end, and everlasting justice be brought, "have been verified throughout the world. And, because all Prophets speak of Christ in the same strain, Daniel continues, "and vision and prophecy may be fulfilled, and the Saint of saints may be anointed," by which we understand the anointing of Jesus Christ, at His Incarnation, with the unction of the Holy Spirit-But, as, at the same time, many different things were accomplished, Daniel describes them all without distinction. He makes mention, first, of "seven weeks," because, in that time, as we read in Esdras and Nehemias, the temple and city, destroyed by Nabuchadonosor, were, with the greatest difficulty, restored. He next speaks of '' sixty-two weeks, "because during that period, as we learn from the book of Maccabees, the Jews were grievously harassed by their enemies. Thirdly, Daniel refers to "one week, "because at the beginning of one week Christ began to preach, and in the middle of a week He was crucified, for He preached for three years and a half. 25

He was followed by His Apostles, who taught the Jews, that the legal sacrifices and ceremonies need no longer be observed, since, as the Reality had come, it was meet that its type should have an end. The doctors of the Church show that Christ began to preach, and was slain, at the predicted lime; and, as men may read their books for themselves, I will pass over the subject briefly. And as the Jews denied Christ before Pilate saying, "we have no king but Caesar, "they were justly condemned by God, and the Gentiles chosen by Him in their stead.

Their rejection is signified by the words, "the people that shall deny Him shall not be His": i.e., in punishment of their sin they were dispersed. Therefore, the Prophet continues, "and a people"— i.e., the Romans — "with their leader that shall come"— i.e., Vespasian and Titus —"shall destroy the city and the sanctuary, "i.e., the Temple. And, as the Jews were completely routed and dispersed, the prophecy concludes with the words, "and the end thereof shall be waste, and after the end of the war the appointed desolation".

God had promised to the Patriarchs and Prophets to send the Messiah, who should open Heaven to them and give them a new law. Thus we read in Jeremias : "Behold the days shall come, says the Lord, and I will make a new covenant with the house of Israel, and with the house of Juda. Not according to the covenant which I made with their fathers, in the day that I took them by the hand to bring them out of the land of Egypt: the covenant which they made void, and I had dominion over them, says the Lord. But this shall be the covenant, that I will make with the house of Israel, after those 'days, says the Lord : I will give My law in their bowels, and I will write it in their heart : and I will be their God, and they shall be My people"(Jer. 31:31-33). Therefore Daniel says, "He shall confirm the covenant with many in one week". This means, that Christ should, by His Blood and His Preaching, with that of His Apostles, confirm the covenant of the New Testament, not to all, (for all would not believe), but to many in one week, the last week, "and in the half of the week the victim and the sacrifice shall fail," because in the middle of this week Jesus Christ was crucified. And, as He was prefigured by the victims and sacrifices of the Old Law, it was meet that when He, the true Light, came, these shadows should flee away. The Temple was thus rendered useless; and by the will of God it was profaned and utterly destroyed.

Therefore Daniel continues, "and there shall be in the temple the abomination of desolation". This abomination signifies, that the statue of the Emperor Hadrian should be set up where the Ark of Moses had stood; for in the eyes of the Jews every idol was. abominable. The expression "abomination "may also refer to the Jewish sacrifices, which were to become abominable before the Lord. Finally, as the Jews will not be converted to the faith, save at the end of the world, 26 Daniel concludes by saying, "the desolation shall continue even to the consummation and to the end".

This is confirmed by the Prophet Osee in the words : "Thou shalt wait for me many days: thou shalt not play the harlot, "i.e., thou shalt not worship idols. This prophecy foretells the fact, that, after their return from Babylon, even to this day, the Jews have not fallen into idolatry, save for a little while at the time of the Maccabees."And thou shalt be no man's, "continues the Prophet, meaning that the Jews should not belong to Christ and I also will wait for thee. For the children of Israel shall sit many days without king, and without prince, and without sacrifice, and without altar, and without ephod, and without teraphim. And after this the children of Israel shall return, and shall seek the Lord their God, and David their King ,"i.e., Christ, the Son of David, "and they shall fear the Lord, and His goodness in the last days"(Osee 3:3, 5).

This prophecy most distinctly points to Jesus of Nazareth. And if we study the other Prophets carefully, we shall see His coming foretold by all. But, returning to our original point, we observe that the time for the advent of the Messiah has already passed, — not only the time determined by the Holy Scriptures, but also the time indicated by many Jewish doctors, — and, as no other man save Jesus of Nazareth, has appeared, bearing the characteristics which were to distinguish the Messiah, everyone must conclude that Christ is the Messiah promised in the Law and the Prophets.

This truth is further borne out by the last Jewish captivity; as we shall see, if we compare it with the Babylonian captivity, by which it is typified. The captivity of Babylon was a punishment to the Jews for their many sins, especially for their idolatry, which of all crimes is the most heinous. Nevertheless, even during their captivity, they were always consoled by the presence of their leaders and prophets and holy men; and their exile did not last for more than seventy years. But their last captivity has lasted for more than 1400 years, which they have passed, deprived of all consolation; without leader, prophet, or holy man. Neither has God assigned any limit to the time of their captivity. Yet, they have not incurred this punishment by idolatry, since, as we have said; they have not, since the Babylonian captivity, fallen into this crime.

Why, then, have the Jews been scattered over the face of the earth? And why has their name been made a byword to all men? Surely, if idolatry be the greatest of all crimes, and if they have not committed it for hundreds of years, their punishment ought to be a lighter one than that which they once incurred for idolatry. They must, then, be suffering for an offence even more heinous. This offence is, that, with malicious perfidy and hatred, they have crucified the true Son of God, whom they knew by His life, His miracles, and the prophecies concerning Him, to be the Messiah. They have, with a few exceptions, persevered in this malice until now. And it is for this crime, and in order to render testimony to our faith, that they have been dispersed over the earth.

Again. For a very long time, no ..sign of sanctity or of true religion has appeared among the Hebrew people. They have been distinguished for avarice and other sins. The gift of prophecy has failed among them. And God does not now, as in times past, show, by any sign, that they are His people. On the other hand, the Church of the Gentiles manifests all holiness of life, true religion, and the wonderful works of Christ and of His saints. Thus is verified the prophecy of Malachy, who, speaking in the person of God, to the Jews, says, "I have no pleasure in you, says the Lord of hosts : and I will not receive a gift of your hand. For from the rising of the sun even to the going down. My name is great among the Gentiles, and in every place there is sacrifice, and there is offered to My name a clean oblation : for My name is great among the Gentiles, says the Lord of hosts"(Mai. 1:10, 11). if God, who is no longer with the Hebrew people, be not with the Gentiles, He must have utterly forsaken the human race.

Again. If it be true that God does not despise small things, neither does He contemn such as are greater. He has foretold by His Prophets many events, such as matters concerning the small kingdoms of the Moabites, Ammonites, far less important than the deeds of Christ and of His Church. Surely, then, it would be an extraordinary thing, were He to pass over in silence these wonderful works; the more so as he made known, before the coming of our Lord, all the evils which have since befallen the Jews. Now, as the Kingdom of Christ was to be to the Jews a far greater and more enduring calamity than any other, is it reasonable to suppose that God, who warned them of the minor evils which would come upon them from Nabuchodonosor, and other kings and nations, would have made no reference in the Scripture to the advent of Christ? But, as the Scriptures do contain abundant mention of Him; and as, by comparing His works with the words of the Prophets, we see that no prophecies can apply to Him, save those that refer to the Messiah, we are driven to conclude, either that God has deceived us, or that Jesus Christ is the Messiah.

If, again, we study history, we shall see, that, before the coming of our Lord, God continually showed forth His wonders among the Jewish people; but since the advent of Christ, no marvelous sign has ever been wrought amongst them. This proves that they are forsaken of God. That the Almighty has abandoned them, is further shown, by the blindness of their understanding. For their doctrines are full of fables so foolish, that no one, with any sense, would propagate them. And their expositions of Holy Scripture are so palpably erroneous, that one wonders that shame has not prevented their publishing, or even conceiving, the fallacies in which they abound.

We might adduce many other proofs in refutation of the Jews. But the doctors of the Church have written very fully on this matter; so, that which we have said about it must suffice. However, if any one will study the arguments just brought forward against the Jews, together with those adduced in our Second Book, he will most certainly conclude, that Jesus of Nazareth is the true God, and the Messiah foretold by the Prophets.

CHAPTER VI.

THE MALICIOUS UNTRUTHFULNESS OF HERETICS.

We must next consider the case of heretics, who, while acknowledging Christ and the Gospel, are involved in many errors. It would take too long to refute every heresy. Therefore, as learned authors have devoted themselves to this task, we will simply, by means of reasoning, confute the principles common to them all.

First, then, we will prove that it is necessary that the Church should be governed by one only head. For, if heretics believe That Divine Providence rules the world, and especially the Church, by which such great deeds have been wrought, they must, to be consistent, admit that the form of government ordained by the Lord of all things must be the best. Now, the best government is a monarchy; because, by it a nation is brought into closer unity, than by a government administered by many; and union and peace are the end aimed at by government. Therefore, as the government of the Church is the best kind of government, its government must be a monarchy.

Again, the government of lower things naturally follows the government of such as are higher; and the more closely it resembles it, the more perfect it will be. Hence, the government of the Church militant, being fashioned on the pattern of that of the Church triumphant, which is ruled by God alone, must be administered by one ruler only.

Further, supernatural things are more perfectly ordered than are things natural. Now in nature we see that wheresoever government exists there is only one ruler; for bees have only one queen, and the limbs of the body are regulated by the heart. Therefore, as the government of the Church, being supernatural, is superior to all other governments, it must be administered by one governor alone.

Now, all heretics agree with us either about the New Testament alone, or about the New Testament and the Old together; although they dissent from us in the interpretation of the Scriptures. But both in the Old and in the New Testament, it is distinctly said that the Church is to have one head."The children of Juda, and the children of Israel shall be gathered together : and they shall appoint themselves under one head, "says Osee (1:11)."There shall be one fold and one Shepherd," says our Lord (St. John 10:16). No one can reasonably understand such words as meaning, that after His ascension, Christ would be the Head of His Church in such sense that no earthly head would be required. For He would thus have created endless confusion and discord; and there would have been no means of adjudicating between the many opinions concerning faith and morals, which would have arisen amongst Christians. Therefore, our Lord, speaking to St. Peter alone, said, "Feed My sheep"(Matt. 21:18). And again, "I have prayed for thee that thy faith fail not : and thou being once converted, confirm thy brethren"(Luke 22:32). Hereby is shown that He left St Peter as His vicar. He proved his intention still more clearly when lie said, "Thou art Peter; and upon this rock I will build My Church, and the gates of hell shall not prevail against it. And I will give to thee the keys of the Kingdom of Heaven. And whatsoever thou shalt bind upon earth, it shall be bound also in Heaven : and whatsoever thou shalt loose on earth, it shall be loosed also in Heaven" (Matt. 16:18, 19).

It cannot, however, be supposed that Christ gave this dignity to St. Peter only, to the exclusion of his successors; since He Himself declared, that the Church should endure forever in the order established by Him. Speaking to His disciples, and addressing, in their person, all the faithful. He said, "Behold I am with you, even unto the consummation of the world" (Matt, 28:20). And again, by the mouth of Isaias, He says, "He shall sit upon the throne of David, and upon his Kingdom : to establish it, and strengthen it with judgment and with justice, from henceforth and for ever"(Is. 9:7). These passages clearly indicate, that the office confided by Christ to St. Peter, being highly expedient and necessary to the Church, should by a perpetual succession, be guaranteed to her forever. Hence it follows that, as St. Peter was chosen by Christ to be His vicar and the shepherd of the whole Church, all his successors must inherit his power. And, as the Bishops of Rome hold the place of Peter, the Roman Church must consequently be the mistress and ruler of all churches; and the whole body of the faithful must be in unity with the Roman Pontiff. Whosoever therefore disagrees in his teaching with the doctrine of the Roman Church, withdraws from Christ, following crooked ways. And, as all heretics dissent from the teaching of the Church, they have all declined from the right way and are unworthy of the name of Christians. For by heretics we mean such as, falsifying the Holy Scripture, and choosing a religion for themselves, do obstinately persevere in their error.

Again, it is often said: "Truth mates with truth, and all truths confirm each other". But heretics disagree so

223

completely between themselves, that they have scarcely a point in common; nay, rather, they are perpetually flinging abuse at one another; and no solid argument can be found in their teaching. This, of itself, proves how far they have strayed from the truth. But the doctrine of the Roman Church, so far as regards faith and morals, is one; and her doctors, "though almost innumerable, never dissent, nor desire to dissent, from it.

Again, the Kingdom of Christ and of the Church militant will endure until the consummation of the world. Nay, more, even after the earth shall have been made new, this kingdom will last forever, in the Church triumphant. Now, as many heretics have risen against the Roman Church, and have been absolutely crushed, it is clear that they cannot have formed part of the Church, and that their teaching was not of God.

Again, the sinful lives of many heretics prove, further, that they come not from God. Not one, even among the most eminent of the heresiarchs, has been held in the veneration accorded to the Saints of our Church, whose very bones and ashes are solemnly honoured, while the day of their death is commemorated by praises of their holy lives.
Heretics also fall into numerous errors not only concerning Holy Scripture, but regarding natural reason and true philosophy. This is another proof that their teaching is not inspired by God. But we need not further discuss their errors, since they have been abundantly refuted by holy doctors. And their heretical doctrines (I speak of those that have more publicly attacked the Church), have been almost entirely extirpated. This itself, is a proof that they came not forth from Got

CHAPTER VII.

THE UTTER IRRATIONALITY OF THE MAHOMETAN RELIGION

MAHOMETANS, who observe the Jewish rite of circumcision and maintain almost every heretical doctrine, stand midway between Jews and heretics. It shall be our last, and not very difficult, task to refute them. I say that the task should not be a difficult one, for any one who knows the religion and reads the Koran of Mahomet, must be at once convinced of the folly of his system. All religion, to be true, must be either supernatural, or must proceed from the light of natural religion.

Now, the Mahometan superstition can be inspired by no wisdom, either human or Divine, seeing that any one, however moderately versed in philosophy, can easily confute it.

The book of the Koran, or collection of precepts, bears ample testimony to the ignorance of its author, Mahomet. Its contents are so confusedly brought together, that no one in the world could, I believe, arrange them. This want of method is a clear sign of ignorance, or of falseness of judgment. But the Koran is also so full of fables and immortality that it deserves ridicule rather than serious analysis. It is evident that such a law could not proceed from natural reason, and still less from supernatural inspiration, since, as we have before shown, what is opposed to natural light, is necessarily opposed also to supernatural wisdom.

Again, a bad beginning rarely, if ever, brings a good ending. Now, Mahometanism began with Mahomet, who, as history tells us, was a most unreasonable and un-principled man, an adulterer, and a robber. He was subject to epileptic fits, which often caused him to fall prostrate, and these falls he attributed to colloquies with an angel. Gradually, and by means, not of argument, but of violence and bribery, he gathered around him a number of uneducated and depraved men; and with their assistance conquered vast multitudes of people. A sect, begun in this fashion, was not likely to have a good end.

Mahomet, in his Koran, approves both the New and the Old Testament. He commends Christ as a true "Prophet, born of the Virgin Mary. But, in spite of this, he accuses Christians of having falsified both the Old and the New Testament. Such an accusation will, easily, be rejected by anyone who considers the uniformity existing between the versions of the Old and New Testament, whether written in Hebrew, Greek, Latin, or any other language, either ancient or modern. Had Christians tampered with the Scriptures, how could the versions of the Bible be uniform? This would be wonderful, existing, as they do, in so many languages, and written in such numbers of books, both Jewish and Christian, ancient and modern. This very uniformity of all the versions of the Scriptures is a clear proof that the fables of Mahomet, and the Koran itself, are but a tissue of lies.

Again, every true religion is established for the purpose of teaching a virtuous mode of life. Its end is the practice of purity of heart. It is intended to facilitate the contemplation of the Divine mysteries. Now, the religion of Mahomet is absolutely material. Completely ignoring true beatitude, it promises to its followers after this life, nothing but the enjoyment of sensual gratification.

There is no ground for saying that Mahomet spoke allegorically. The Koran contains no explanation of any parable, such as are to be found in our Scriptures.

Among the Mahometans, again, we do not, as in the Christian religion, meet with any miracles, or manifestation of Divine phenomena. Mahomet while acknowledging Christ as the messenger of God, commissioned to convert the world by miracles, said that he himself had been sent by Heaven to convert it by the sword. This pretension was obviously ridiculous; since God takes no pleasure in tyranny, nor in compulsory service. There is nothing striking in the doctrine contained in the Koran; yet the Mahometans think that they are uttering a wonderful saying, when they pronounce the words, "There is but one God, and Mahomet is His prophet"; "God is great and powerful". This, and similar phrases, are often repeated, and to them are added fables, which our very children would ridicule.

Again, the Mahometans, unlike Christians, own no prophets, no holy men, no workers of heavenly wonders.

They venerate as saints, certain madmen, who mutilate their bodies, perform strange antics, and know nothing of Divine things. Mahomet also, constantly contradicts himself in his Koran. He says that he knows not, whether he and his followers are in the way of salvation; and that he believes, that none can understand his law. It is a matter of surprise to me, that he was not stoned by his own people for giving them an unintelligible code, and leaving them in doubt about their salvation. His law indeed, being supported neither by natural reason, by miracles, nor by sanctity of life, is, fittingly, an object of derision. If Mahomet had attempted to establish his religion by preaching, his errors would have been very easily demonstrated. But, knowing that his doctrine was indefensible on any logical grounds, he had the astuteness to command, that it should be propagated by the sword.

It may surprise some persons that Mahomet should have been successful in perverting so many nations, and in seducing them from Christ. For, it may be thought that Mahomet had greater influence than our Lord, the more so as his kingdom has constantly been on the increase. Our answer is, that there is nothing in this fact, which ought to impair our belief in the Christian religion. It does not, in the least, diminish the strength of the arguments which we have already adduced to prove the Divinity of its Founder. For neither in the law of Mahomet, nor in any other religious system, can anything be discovered, more holy, or more wonderful, than the Christian dogmas.

As for the fact of Mahomet's having withdrawn many from Christianity, as much may be asserted of the devil. So, this is no proof of Mahomet's superiority to Christ. For Satan has conquered a far greater multitude of souls than either our Lord or Mahomet have gained. If numbers are to be considered as a testimony to truth, we ought to follow in the wake of impious men, rather than to imitate the piety of the just. Bad men will always outnumber the good. It is indeed a surprising mode of arguing in favour of Mahomet, to say, that he must be superior to Christ, because, by means of the sword, he has subjected many to his irrational and degrading law. Such are not our arguments; nor was the Mahometan system that on which Christianity was founded. Small wonder is it, that Jesus has so few followers, since He commands us to live virtuously, to suffer until death, and yet, promises us none but invisible rewards. If the reasoning of those who uphold Mahometanism were correct, it would gainsay, not only supernatural doctrine, but also philosophy. For the conclusion, logically arising from it, is, that good is evil; truth, falsehood; and light, darkness. For, if the fact that a system is followed by a multitude renders it true and good and luminous; and if, as is the case, the number of men living virtuously and reasonably is extremely small, all our notions of religion and morality must be reversed.

Again, we must remember that, as God allows those who will not walk in the truth to be blinded. He suffered certain nations, as a punishment for their sins, to be seduced by Mahomet. Surely, had such not been His will, and had these races not deserved such a chastisement, Mahomet would have been powerless. For, if Christ was able, whilst His Name was still unknown, and the world was full of idolatry, to convert, by peaceful means, so many nations to Himself, how much more glorious would be His triumph, now that His Name is magnified throughout the whole earth? But, as we have just said, God allowed certain nations to be infected by Mahometanism, to punish them for their sins. Such a judgment is consistent with the words of our Lord, "Many are called, but few are chosen"(Matt. 20:16).

We must, likewise, remember that the Church has frequently increased numerically, and frequently diminished, because ma n possesses free will, and because God does not force him to virtue, but draws him by love. He either promises him eternal happiness, or threatens him, if he persist in sin, with divers penalties, of which one of the chief is the darkening of his understanding. Thus, David,

229

speaking in the person of Christ, and of the just against the wicked, says, "Let their eyes be darkened that they see not; and their back bend thou down always"(Ps. 68:24). Again, we find in Isaias,
"Blind the heart of this people, and make their ears heavy, and shut their eyes : lest they see with their eyes, and hear with their ears, and understand with their heart, and be converted, and I heal them" (Isa. 6:10). This blindness of heart and stubbornness of mind, foretold by the Prophets, was the first punishment that overtook the Jews.

We know, also, that it has been predicted, that many are to fall away from the faith. Our Lord, speaking of the end of the world says ,"Because iniquity has abounded, the charity of many has grown cold" (Matt. 24:12). He says again, "The Son of Man, when He comes, shall He find, think you, faith on earth"? (Luke 18:8). St. Paul, likewise, writes thus to Timothy, "Now the Spirit manifestly says, that in the last times some shall depart from the faith, giving heed to spirits of error, and doctrines of devils"(1 Tim. 4:1). And, if we study the teaching of the Gospel, we shall find that this blindness of heart, the severest of all punishments, because it leads to hell, has been "foretold by Christ, and by Him has been permitted to overtake men for their ingratitude and malice.

Someone may, however, reply, that it does not seem just that children should be punished for the sins of their fathers; and that if the Jews and Mahometans offended God, them indeed He ought to have punished with blindness, but not to have involved in the same fate their descendants. To this argument we would reply, that, as the faith of Christ is known to the entire world, no one can

be excused for disbelieving it. Of course, children would not be punished with their fathers, if they did not commit their fathers' sins. Men are all the less excusable, since, if they lived according to natural reason, and prayed to God for their eternal salvation, they would most undoubtedly be enlightened by faith. For, although we know that the judgments of God are unsearchable, we know likewise that He will never be wanting to any creature in its necessity. The Apostle says, "For God has concluded all in unbelief, that He may have mercy on all". Then, contemplating the unfathomable abyss of the Divine Majesty he immediately continues, "O the depth of the riches, of the wisdom, and of the knowledge of God! How incomprehensible are His judgments,
and how unsearchable His ways! For who has known the mind of the Lord? Or who has been His coun-sellor? Or who has first given to Him, and recompense shall be made him? For of Him, and by Him, and in Him, are all things : to Him be glory forever, Amen" (Rom. 11:32-36).

We must, nevertheless, bear in mind that Christ our Lord, who foretold these evils to come, has likewise assured us that His Church shall never fail. For "behold," He says, "I am with you always, even unto the consummation of the world". Now, as the calamities which He prophesied have come to pass, we have every reason to trust that the blessing which He has promised will also be vouchsafed to us. We may say this with confidence, as the Church is so solidly established, that it is folly to think that She can fail. We trust, therefore, that, as Christ has punished unfaithful Christians, He will like- wise make new His Church, opening to her the whole world, that, so, there may be '' one fold and one Shepherd". This, we know, will quickly come to pass. And, thus, the ship of Peter will plough her way forward, sometimes borne on by favouring winds, and sometimes buffeted by storms. But the law of Mahomet, based not on reason, Divine or human, but on physical force, cannot endure; for nothing established by violence can continue.

CHAPTER VIII.

THE CHRISTIAN RELIGION WILL REMAIN TRUE AND UNWAVERING UNTO THE END.

As all religion must proceed either from natural reason, from supernatural light, or from the union of the two, we should be bound, if there existed any religions or superstitions besides these that we have enumerated, to refute them with the same arguments that we have already used. For all religions founded by men, enlightened merely by natural light, are based, as is the religion of the ancient philosophers, on the true principles of human reason. We have already shown that such a religion will not suffice for salvation. Such religions may be founded on false principles of reason. This may occur in one of two ways. They may be as is the superstition of astrology, grounded on false principles concerning natural things; or, like idolatry, on false principles emanating from Satan. Further, no religion can exist proceeding from supernatural light which is not established on the Old and the New Testament together, A false religion may, like the Jewish, be based on the Old Testament alone; or, like heretical sects, on misinterpretation of the New Testament; or, like Mahometanism, it may rest on a medley of the Old and the New Testaments. But Christianity is founded on both the Testaments, and is illuminated both by natural reason and by supernatural light. Since then the religions which we have enumerated, — to wit, philosophy, astrology, idolatry, Judaism, heresy, and Mahometanism, — are the chief religions in the world; and since Christianity surpasses them, both in reasonableness, in miracles, and in all other ways, as immeasurably as Heaven dominates earth, or light darkness; it is plain, that Christianity must be the true religion, and the sure harbour of salvation.

But to forestall caviling, we will add that, even should someone proclaim the advent into the world of a religion superior to the Christian Faith, this would in no wise dim the glory of Christianity. Firstly, because, as, at present, no better religion than that of Christ exists, we ought to follow it until a better appear. Secondly, because it is unreasonable to think, that a religion, superior to Christianity, can exist. For, as the Faith of Christ sets before us the best possible end, the surest possible means of attaining thereto, the most perfect life, and the greatest and most wonderful deeds, it can never be superseded by any other system.

But, supposing, for the sake of argument, that a religion, superior to Christianity, should arise, it would not condemn our Faith. For, since Christianity, as we have shown, proceeds from supernatural light; and since it is, in no wise, opposed to that which is natural, it can have come from none but God. Thus, it can be condemned by no other religion. Any better religion than Christianity must approve and commend the Christian Faith; because any such reaction would, necessarily, arise either from natural or supernatural light. From whichever of these sources it might spring, such a religion would, necessarily, approve and commend Christianity. For truth must be ever in harmony with truth; and whatever arises from natural or supernatural light, must proceed from God the Creator of this dual light, which, by its beams, enlightens the world with His truth. Were natural and supernatural light opposed to each other, one would necessarily be false; and God would teach men at one time falsehood, and at another time truth. This hypothesis is manifestly absurd. For, were God thus to confuse our understanding, we should be incapable of knowing the truth. To produce such a condition in His creatures is foreign to the Divine Nature. Therefore, if any other true religion were to arise in the world, it would be, of necessity, bound to approve Christianity, and to commend it as the truth which leads to eternal life.

CHAPTER IX.

EPILOGUE.

Arguments carry greatest weight when accumulated.
Therefore, the conclusion of our work shall consist of a
brief summary of the line of argument pursued throughout it. We will begin, therefore, by asserting that the
faith of Christians in the teaching of Christ, and their
observance of His commandments, is not founded on
frivolous motives, but on the most prudent grounds.
Every intelligent man who considers the greatness and
the wondrous harmony of the universe, will be convinced,
that there must be a God, the Supreme Cause and Primary
Mover of all things For, as everything that
moves is moved by some other thing, there must be
some First Mover. Further, spirit being more noble
than body, and God being noble above all things, He
must be a spirit and simple substance, or Pure Act.
Hence it follows, that He is perfect, Supreme Good,
Supreme Power, Immutable, Eternal, One. All that is
noble is, in proportion to its elevation above matter,
more fully endowed with knowledge. God, therefore,
must be Highest Intelligence, and possessed of free-will.

He must act, not out of necessity, but by means of His
Will. As, by means of His Intelligence and Will, He
acts in all things, even in the very least, we must
acknowledge that His providence cares for all things, and
especially for man, for whom He has created . every
natural thing. Hence, it pertains to God, to guide man
to his last end, to wit, the contemplation of Divine things.

But, as such beatitude cannot be attained in this present
life, wherein we are encompassed by misery, and enjoy

but scant knowledge of God, we are forced, under pain
of being very inconsistent, to believe in another life, and
to maintain that the soul is immortal, and that it is the form
of the body. Thus the Catholic Church, with respect to the
natural order of things, teaches, about God and the final
blessedness of man, naught save what is most reasonable
and intelligible.

If we next call to mind the picture which I drew of
the Triumph of the Cross, we shall see that Christians,
in confessing the faith of Christ, show the truest wisdom.
For, the necessity of the existence of some religion in the
world cannot be denied, when man's natural tendency to
religion — the means whereby blessedness is attained — is
taken into account. And, if the end of religion be a good
life, and a good life be that true religion whereby God IS
perfectly honoured, then as no better life than the Christian
life exists, we must confess Christianity to be the true
religion, whereby man is surely led to blessedness.

If it be a hard matter to believe that Jesus Christ,
who was crucified, is both God and Man, we must bear
in mind, that, were this article of Faith an error, it could
not produce, foster, and develop the Christian life. Yet,
as a matter of fact, this truth produces, more than
does any other article of our belief, consummate perfection among Christians. Again, we know that the
Holy Scriptures of the Old and New Testament, on
which our whole creed is founded, must be from God.
Otherwise, the innumerable events which they predict
would not have been verified; nor would the Scriptures
have borne such abundant fruit throughout the world.

If our Faith were false, men of purified intellect could not
fail, especially when they are engaged in contemplation and

prayer, to discern its errors; but, contrariwise, we see that such men are the boldest champions of the Faith.

Again, were our religion false, its exterior rites could not, as they do, sanctify those who practice them reverently, nor deprave those who desecrate them. Neither, were the Faith untrue, could it give to the hearts of Christians such peace, and joy, and freedom, as to make them account affliction as a blessing and consolation; nor would it beautify their very countenance with such an expression of sincerity and calm, as to render them venerable in the sight of all men, and a powerful attraction to the practice of Christian virtue.

Furthermore, when we consider the power of Christ, whereby He has overcome all — gods, emperors, tyrants, philosophers, heretics, and barbarous nations; when we remember how His work has been accomplished — not by the sword, nor by wealth, nor by human wisdom, but by the daily torture and death of His martyrs; when we think of His Divine Wisdom which has so speedily enlightened the world and purged it of its errors; and when we reflect upon His mercy, whereby He has attracted multitudes to His love so powerfully, that not only have they renounced all earthly possessions, but have gladly suffered martyrdom rather than deny one jot or tittle of the faith — can we hesitate as to the truth of Christianity? What god, or what man has wrought like wonders? If these marvelous works have been performed without a miracle; this, of itself, would be the greatest of miracles. But if they have been wrought miraculously, these miracles prove that Christianity is blessed by God.

If we next study the teaching of Christ, we shall see that it contains nothing unreasonable. The very mystery of the Blessed Trinity is imaged forth in creatures. It is reasonable, again, to believe that God is the Creator of all things, since everything needs an efficient cause. Likewise, since man is created for supernatural happiness, it is logical to maintain the sanctification and glory of the soul, and the resurrection of the body; for without the body, the soul would be imperfect. Furthermore, in order that the senses, more especially the eyes, of glorified bodies, may have more perfect and more fitting objects on which to exercise themselves, it is rational to believe that this earth will likewise be glorified. As God is able to do more than we can conceive. He was able by His power to become man. And it was most fitting that He should become incarnate, in order to instruct mankind as to its final beatitude, as to the true means for its attainment, and also, that He might make satisfaction to the Eternal Father for the sins of men. It beseemed Him, likewise, to be born of a Spotless Virgin, and to die upon the Cross, to teach us to face even death for justice' sake. It was meet, too, that in order to give us hopes of our resurrection. He should rise again, and that, having been unjustly judged by the wicked. He should become the Judge of the living and the dead.

Again, nothing can be more in accordance with reason, than is the judicial and ethical code of Christianity; since no life is so perfect as is the Christian life. This results from the government of the Church, whose doctrines contain all that is best in the teaching of philosophers and sages. There is, again, nothing unreasonable, or absurd, in ecclesiastical ceremonies. This evidenced
by the sanctity of life, resulting from devout observance of them.

Where, then, shall we find a religion, established on such solid grounds of reason, as is Christianity? Philosophers ignored the true end of human life. Astrology is a web of superstition. Idolatry contains neither morality nor truth. Judaism is refuted by its prophets of old, and by the present captivity of its followers. The discord among heretics, and the extermination of their sects, is a strong proof that they are in error. Mahometanism outrages every principle of philosophy. Christianity alone is resplendent with natural and supernatural light; and is adorned by sanctity, wisdom, miracles, and wondrous deeds.

Can any intelligent man, then, refrain from devoutly embracing the Faith of Christ? Can anyone fail to perceive the rashness and folly of those who revile a religion, blessed by God, and preserved by Him through centuries of persecution, and consecrated by the blood of innumerable martyrs? Surely, every man of sound judgment acknowledges Christianity to be true. Every man must believe that there exists another life, into which all must pass; that each one of us must stand before the awful Judge who will place on His left hand the wicked condemned to eternal punishment, and, on His right, the good who will enter into everlasting bliss. In this glory unutterable they shall gaze forever on. God in Trinity unspeakable, infinite. They shall rejoice in the grace of our all-conquering and triumphant Lord and Saviour, Jesus Christ, to whom be power, and divinity, and wisdom, and strength, and honour, forever and ever. AMEN

FOOTNOTES:

1 Life of St. Philip Neri, translated by Father Pope, vol. 1., p. 278.

2 Tome 1., p. 885. Edit. Paris, 1719.

3 This will account for some few slight and unimportant verbal variations from the original Latin edition in the present English translation, which, though it has been compared with the Latin, has been made from the Italian version.

4 Many other editions were afterwards printed In Italy and elsewhere, which are not mentioned by Echard.

5 Page 339. Edit. Paris, 1879.

6 An imperfect edition in English appeared in 1661. A copy is to be found in the Cambridge University Library. It was "printed by John Field, printer to the University, Cambridge, "under the title, "The Truth of the Christian Faith; or, The Triumph of the Cross, by Hieronymus Savonarola, done into English out of the author's own Italian copy"; and it was dedicated '' To the much honoured Francis S. John, Esq.".

7 The alphabetical Index at the end of this translation is not found in either the Latin or the Italian edition. It is added for the convenience of the English reader.

8 Page 235.

9 Heb. 13:8.

10 Isa. 59:21.

11 In addition to the instances which I shall give later on, the reader will look in vain in Mr. Travers Hill's translation for the reference to '' the blessed Mother of God, the Virgin Mary, "the "Host,""Chalice," "Mary, "and "Relics, "which will be found in chapter 2 of the First Book in this translation (and in the original, which Mr. Hill professes to reproduce in English). In the

following chapter he will also fail to find Savonarola's words about "Virgins,""the Eucharist,""the
Veneration of the Cross, "and "the reverence due to Mary
and the Saints'". In the eleventh chapter of the Second
Book the subjects of cloistral-life, fasting and watching,
and the three vows of religious, which are found in the
original, are suppressed in the "translation", In the
thirteenth chapter of the same Book, after the words "born
of the Virgin Mary, "the author adds, "Whom He wishes to
be reverenced (quam vult adorari) as the
true Mother of God"; the translator omits the words. Later
on, in the same chapter, Savonarola, writing of the Blessed
Sacrament—"My Body and Blood under the appearance of
bread and wine"— says :"They shall
most devoutly venerate It". (In the Italian edition
Savonarola expresses it "they shall adore It as God"), not
so the "translator"; nor does he insert Savonarola's words
:"My Virgin Mother shall be honoured, "which
immediately follow the reference to the Blessed Sacrament.
The profession of faith in the Roman Catholic Church,
which the reader of this volume will find at the end of the
tenth chapter of the Third Book, and
which begins: "Therefore, the Catholic faith most fittingly,
"etc. (see page 127), is ignored completely by Mr. Hill, but
is found word for word in Savonarola's original work. In
one place (Book 2, chap, 13.) the
words, relating to the Eucharist :"In Ipsius Corpus et
Sanguinem transmutari" are rendered "represent His body
and blood"!

12 See Savonarola and the Reformation — a Reply to
Dean Farrar, by the present writer (Catholic Truth Society).
13 First Epistle of Peter 3:15.
14 Given by Quetif, Annales O. P., vol. 2, p. 125. An
English translation of the letter is to be found in Savonarola
and the Reformation, before referred to, at page 114.

15 "When we look up to the sky and contemplate the heavenly bodies, what can be so evident and so clear, as the existence of a Deity, with a most marvelous mind, by whom all these bodies are governed?"
(Cicero, De Natura Deorum, lib. 2.) — Editor.

16 E.g., St. Ignatius the Martyr, St. Polycarp, St. Clement of Alexandria, etc. — Editor.

17 As this expression occurs frequently in the following pages, it may be well, for the uninitiated in scholastic phraseology, to explain its meaning. Savonarola, in the 10th chapter of this 1st Book, defines Pure Act as
being ''superior to all matter and possibility," and in the 2nd chapter of the following Book, He writes: "God is not a body, but Pure Act". The term Pure Act is applied to the Most High by theologians, to exclude all
imperfection, and all possibility of change, or of any further acquisition. St. Thomas in his Summa Theologica (Pars prima, Quaest. 25. art. I) distinguishes between that which is in actu, and that which is in potentia.
To say of anything that it is in potentia (or possibility) implies that it may still receive something, or become something which it has not or is not, something which it lacks; and that, therefore, it is wanting and imperfect (deficiens et imperfectum) — e.g., a child is in potentia to become a man — he may someday be a man; or an ignorant man is in potentia to learning — he may become a learned man; there is a possibility of it —
therefore, as yet, he is imperfect. In actu, on the other hand, means that it actually possesses some special gift or perfection. God has everything that He possibly can have. He is everything that He possibly can be in
the scale of perfection — nothing is wanting to Him, nothing further is possible to Him. Hence St. Thomas concludes: "God is Pure Act simply and universally perfect; nor is there any imperfection in Him"

(ibid.). No creature can be called Pure Act; because every creature is potentia — he may receive or become something which he has not or is not. The term is applied to God alone. — Editor.

18 De Simplicitate Vitae Christiana. This little work consists of five short treatises, or, as the author calls them, "Books". It is from the pen of Savonarola himself. It was first published in Italian at Florence
in the year 1496, and afterwards, in Latin, at Venice, and at the Ascension Press in Paris. As the title suggests, it treats of certain practical and simple rules, which help souls to attain to the perfection of the Christian life. I do not know of any existing English translation of this booklet. —Editor,

19 The author, probably, had in his mind the dream of Nabuchadonosor, interpreted by the prophet Daniel (Dan. 2.). — Editor.

20 See Introduction, p. 10.

21 The reader will, naturally, recall the words of St. Thomas, in the Lauda Sion : —

"Fracto demum Sacramento,
Ne vacilles, sed memento,
Tantum esse sub fragmento,
Quantum toto tegitur,"etc.,

of which the late Father Aylward, 0,P., has left the following translation : —

"When the priest the Victim breaketh,
See thy faith it nowise shaketh;
Know that every fragment taketh
All that 'neath the whole there lies;

This in Him no fracture maketh,
'Tis the figure only breaketh.

Form or state, no change there taketh
Place, in what it signifies."— Editor.

22   i.e., in Italian. It was published in Florence in the year
1495. Afterwards a Latin edition, Contra Astrologiam
Divinatricem lib. 3, was printed. — Editor.

23   i.e., angels, or else disembodied spirits, or souls which
have left this world; to some of which pagans gave Divine
worship. — Editor.

24   i.e. Divine worship. — Editor,

25   The author, quoting the Book of Leviticus, has already
said (p. 183), that the "week "of Daniel's prophecy is to
be interpreted as being a week of years. He here reminds
his readers that in the middle of the week our Lord was
crucified, i.e., after three years and a half (or halt of seven
years) preaching."He shall confirm His covenant with
many, in one week : and in the half of the week the victim
and sacrifice shall fail "(Dan. 9:27). — Editor.

26   Probably a reference to St. Paul's words : ' For I would
not have you ignorant, brethren, of this mystery (lest you
should be wise in your own conceits), that blindness in part
has happened in Israel, until the fullness of the Gentiles
shall come in. And so all Israel should be saved, as it is
written : there shall come out of Sion, He that shall deliver,
and shall turn away impiety from Jacob. . . . According to
the Gospel, indeed,
they are enemies for your sake : but according to election
they are most dear for the sake of the fathers"(Rom. 11:25,
26, 28). Editor.

END

Other Titles Offered by St Athanasiuis Press
http://www.stathanasiuspress.com

The 1957 Edition of The Raccolta
or A Manual of Indulgences

Vera Sapentia or True Wisdom
by Thomas A Kempis

The Valley of Lilies & The Little Garden of Roses
by Thomas A Kempis

A Thought From Thomas A Kempis
for Each Day of the Year

The History of Heresies and Their Refutation
by St Alphonsus Liguori, C.SS.R.

Treatise on Prayer
by St Alphonsus Liguori, C.SS.R.

The Dignity and Duties of the Priest or Selva
by St Alphonsus Liguori, C.SS.R.

3 Volume Set
The Practice of Christian and Religious Perfection
by Fr Alphonsus Rodriguez, S.J.

1910 Benziger Catalog
Church Ornaments or our own Manufacture

The Eternal Happiness of the Saints
by St Robert Bellarmine

Devotion to the Nine Choirs of Holy Angels
by Henri Marie Boudon

We also have 120+ Catholic ebooks for sale
at Amazon's Kindle Store
Search for "st athanasius press"
in Kindle to find our ebooks there

To find us on Twitter search for: wallmell

www.ingramcontent.com/pod-product-compliance
Lightning Source LLC
Chambersburg PA
CBHW021223090426
42740CB00006B/347